KU-026-745

50 WALKS IN
North Yorkshire

50 WALKS OF 2–10 MILES

Contents

Contents

Rating

Each walk is rated for its relative difficulty compared to the other walks in this book. Walks marked ✦✦✦ are likely to be shorter and easier with little total ascent. The hardest walks are marked ✦✦✦.

Walking in Safety

For advice and safety tips see page 144.

Locator Map

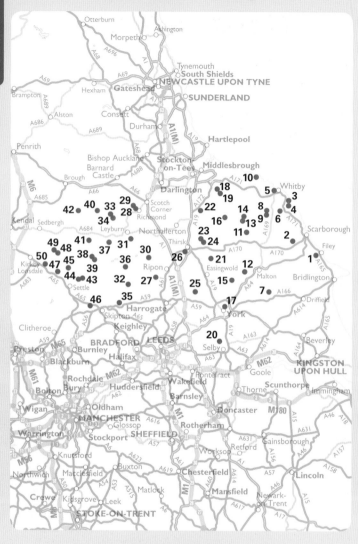

Legend

—→—	Walk Route	▨	Built-up Area
❶	Route Waypoint	▨	Woodland Area
— — —	Adjoining Path	🚻	Toilet
⚡	Viewpoint	🅿	Car Park
●	Place of Interest	🏕	Picnic Area
⌂	Steep Section	)(	Bridge

Introducing
North Yorkshire

If you were to draw a straight line from North Yorkshire's most easterly point, just north of Flamborough Head, to its most westerly, near Low Bentham, it would stretch nearly 100 miles (161km). From north to south is 65 miles (105km). The county stretches from the North Sea to within 10 miles (16km) of Morecambe Bay on the west coast. It is a huge area – England's largest county.

It is also one of the most rural, with historic York as the only sizeable city. Its two National Parks, the Yorkshire Dales and the North York Moors, occupy much of the two ends of the county. The Howardian Hills, south of the Moors, and Nidderdale, south-east of the Dales, are designated Areas of Outstanding Natural Beauty. In its far south-eastern corner, North Yorkshire also takes in part of the Wolds.

So this is prime walking country, from the heather-clad heights of the North York Moors to the limestone country that is typical of the Yorkshire Dales – a place of contrasts and discoveries, history and legend.

Walking is the best way to see North Yorkshire. Large areas are unvisited by roads, and some of the best landscape is only accessible on foot. In the North York Moors the roads tend to follow the tops of the ridges, leaving hidden valleys and deep forest to be discovered. The east coast, with its compact fishing villages, like Staithes and Robin Hood's Bay, and its towering cliffs, is best discovered from the Cleveland Way, which also takes you in a huge sweep around the northern fringes of the National Park. Here, too, are castles, like Helmsley and Pickering, and the ruins of great abbeys, like Rievaulx and Byland, as well as the great Castle Howard estate. There are minor pleasures to discover, too – for example, the crosses of the North York Moors – once beacons for travellers as well as memorials – and the remains of ironstone mining.

Further south, across the Vale of Pickering, once a huge lake, is the very different landscape of the Wolds. Here, deep, dry chalk valleys and ancient earthworks are part of the attraction – as is the timeless, quiet feel of this little-known area. Moving west across the centre of the county, an area of rich agricultural land dotted with market towns like Thirsk and Bedale, as well as the cathedral city of Ripon and the spa town of Harrogate, you come to Nidderdale and then the Dales National Park. Nidderdale is a

PUBLIC TRANSPORT

It is possible to use public transport to reach the starting point of some of these walks. Railway lines radiate from York to Scarborough, Thirsk and Northallerton, Harrogate and Selby. Whitby is accessible via the Esk Valley line, which connects with the North Yorkshire Moors Railway. In the west, the Settle-to-Carlisle line provides access to some of the most spectacular Dales country. Buses, too, have become more user-friendly and, in the summer, provide a regular service to many of the main tourist spots. For more information go to www.yorkshiretravel.net or call Traveline on 0871 200 22 33.

tough but spectacular landscape with reservoirs and the remains of lead mining. But for many visitors, it is the Yorkshire Dales that leave the most vivid memories. This is a landscape of caverns and waterfalls, limestone pavements and wooded valleys, sheep-cropped grass and the gaunt remains of industry, softened over time. Stone-built villages cluster round ancient bridges or surround wide greens. Huge crags – none greater than Malham Cove – and deep gorges – like the Cove's great neighbour Gordale Scar – will impress you with the force and grandeur of nature. Here, too, as on the North York Moors, you will be struck by the ancient place-names, many deriving from the Norse and Danish settlers who long occupied the area.

At all seasons, and in most weathers, North Yorkshire holds its fascination and you can be sure of good food, a warm welcome and great walking!

Using this book

Information Panels

An information panel for each walk shows its relative difficulty (see page 5), the distance and total amount of ascent. An indication of the gradients you will encounter is shown by the rating ▲ ▲ ▲ (no steep slopes) to ▲ ▲ ▲ (several very steep slopes).

Maps

There are 30 maps, covering 40 of the walks. Some walks have a suggested option in the same area. The information panel for these walks will tell you how much extra walking is involved. On short-cut suggestions the panel will tell you the total distance if you set out from the start of the main walk. Where an option returns to the same point on the main walk, just the distance of the loop is given. Where an option leaves the main walk at one point and returns to it at another, then the distance shown is for the whole walk. The minimum time suggested is for reasonably fit walkers and doesn't allow for stops. Each walk has a suggested map.

Start Points

The start of each walk is given as a six-figure grid reference prefixed by two letters indicating which 100km square of the National Grid it refers to. You'll find more information on grid references on most Ordnance Survey maps.

Dogs

We have tried to give dog owners useful advice about how dog friendly each walk is. Please respect other countryside users. Keep your dog under control, especially around livestock, and obey local bylaws and other dog control notices.

Car Parking

Many of the car parks suggested are public, but occasionally you may find you have to park on the roadside or in a lay-by. Please be considerate when you leave your car, ensuring that access roads or gates are not blocked and that other vehicles can pass safely.

Right: Kilburn White Horse viewed across countryside from Whinny Bank in Coxwold (Walk 23)

Gristhorpe Man and his Landscape

A walk in North Yorkshire's eastern extremity,
where prehistoric man lived and died.

DISTANCE 3.75 miles (6km)   MINIMUM TIME 2hrs

ASCENT/GRADIENT 249ft (75m) ▲▲▲   LEVEL OF DIFFICULTY ✛✛✛

PATHS Field paths and tracks, muddy after rain, 4 stiles

LANDSCAPE Hillside, then flat farmland

SUGGESTED MAP OS Explorer 301 Scarborough, Bridlington
& Flamborough Head

START/FINISH Grid reference: TA 096796

DOG FRIENDLINESS Livestock in fields, so dogs on lead

PARKING Street parking in Muston, near the Ship Inn

PUBLIC TOILETS None en route

A little inland from the rocky peninsula of Filey Brigg, which marks the end (or the start) of both the Cleveland Way and the Wolds Way, is peaceful pasture and arable land bounded on the south by the first slopes of the chalk escarpment of the Yorkshire Wolds. It is fertile land, once wet with bog but long-since drained and farmed. The local name for this landscape – 'Carr' – is from an Old Norse word meaning boggy ground.

Early Inhabitants

Some of Britain's earliest inhabitants lived around here – not, like their successors, on the Wolds themselves, but in refuges among the reeds and willows. Most of the details of their civilisation have long since disappeared, with burial sites vanishing under the plough. Fortunately, however, we know much about one inhabitant, now known as Gristhorpe Man, whose remains, along with the artefacts associated with him, are now impressively displayed and interpreted in the Rotunda Museum in the centre of Scarborough.

Gristhorpe Man

In 1834 workmen, employed by the local landowner William Beswick in Gristhorpe, dug into an ancient burial mound on the Carrs near the village. Under a covering of oak branches they uncovered a coffin lid carved with a face (which they later trampled on and made unrecognisable!). The coffin was made from a single oak log, with lichened bark still adhering to it. Inside was the complete skeleton of a man, more than six feet tall, with his legs drawn up to his chest. His body had been wrapped in fine animal skin, secured by a bone pin. With him were a bronze dagger head and a bone pommel for it, as well as a flint knife. By his side was a bark dish stitched with strips of animal skin or sinew. It is believed that he is probably more than 4000 years old, and is likely to have been a Bronze Age chieftain, who died in his forties.

MUSTON

You will get a fine view of Gristhorpe Man's homeland from the first part of the walk as you ascend from Muston on to the slopes of Flotmanby Wold. This is part of the long distance Wolds Way, which runs 79.5 miles (128km) from Hessle Haven on the banks of the Humber to Filey Brigg. If the weather is decent, you will be able to see the Brigg to the north-east while, further to the north, Scarborough is clearly visible.

The Carrs

The walk descends along an ancient hollow way route; this may once have been part of a major prehistoric route from the Wolds on to the watery peat landscape of The Carrs. Today The Carrs are criss-crossed with drainage ditches that include the evocatively-named Old Scurf and the channelled River Hertford, which was cut in 1807. To the north is the Hull-to-Scarborough railway line; there was a railway station just south-west of Gristhorpe village. The walk continues by the Main Drain and alongside Muston Bottoms to the village, which is worth exploring for its range of excellent vernacular houses, many built of chalk, with their typical pantiled roofs.

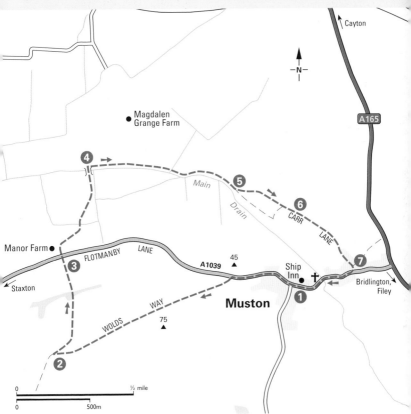

WALK 1 DIRECTIONS

❶ From the Ship Inn, walk in the direction of Folkton. After the houses end, and just before the stone holding the Muston village sign on the right, take a waymarked stile in the hedge on

your left, signed 'Wolds Way'.
Go forward with the hedge on
your right. The path becomes
a track. Follow the Wolds Way
signs uphill over two waymarked
stiles, passing two disused stiles on
the ascent. At the top right-hand
corner of the next field go over
a stile and continue ahead to the
next signpost.

WHERE TO EAT AND DRINK

The walk begins and ends at the
Ship Inn in Muston, which offers
bar meals and snacks, as well
as traditional Sunday lunches.
Just to the north, the Bull Inn at
the eastern end of Gristhorpe
village also offers meals and
snacks, and welcomes children.

2 Go over the embankment
then turn right down the track,
following the bridleway sign.
Continue downhill, in this hollow
way. It comes into a field, which
you walk straight across to reach a
main road, Flotmanby Lane.

3 Cross the road and walk
through the farm buildings of
Manor Farm, bearing right along
the track by a barn. The track
eventually bears left and crosses
a stream, then reaches a drainage
channel that is crossed by a
concrete bridge with metal rails.

4 Cross the bridge and turn
right at the end, along the side

WHAT TO LOOK OUT FOR

Visit Filey Brigg, the rocky
promontory that punctuates
the coast between Flamborough
Head and the castle-crowned
headland at Scarborough. You
can explore the rock pools
for shellfish and small marine
creatures, and reflect on visits
by Charlotte Brontë and by RD
Blackmore, who set part of his
novel *Mary Anerley* here.

WHAT TO LOOK OUT FOR

The soil under your feet will
tell you a great deal about the
geology of this easternmost part
of North Yorkshire. On the first
part of the walk you will find the
light, drier soils that are typical of
the chalk landscape of the Wolds
– sometimes chalk nodules can
be found on the surface. By
contrast, The Carrs has rich, in
places almost black, peat soils.
When the fields north of Manor
Farm in The Ings and Muston
Carr have been newly ploughed
they have the appearance of an
intensely inky landscape.

of the channel. Follow the track
to the next bridge. Do not cross,
but continue straight ahead, still
following the channel. Go through
a waymarked gate and continue
ahead; the drainage channel
eventually swings right, away from
the path. Continue through two
more waymarked gates.

5 Before you reach another
waymarked gate, turn left. Walk
up the field side with the hedge
to your right. Follow the hedge
as it bends round to the right.
The path reaches a waymarked
gate. Go through the gate into
a track called Carr Lane.

6 Follow Carr Lane between
the hedges and past farm
buildings. Eventually the lane
becomes metalled and passes
a row of houses to reach a
T-junction before a green.

7 Turn right, then right again
at the main road. Follow the
main street of Muston as it winds
through the village, past All Saints
Church, to the Ship Inn.

Through Scarborough's Raincliffe Woods

*Just outside Scarborough, a walk through woodland
to the rare remains of a glacial lake.*

DISTANCE *5 miles (8km)*   MINIMUM TIME *2hrs*

ASCENT/GRADIENT *584ft (178m)* ▲▲▲   LEVEL OF DIFFICULTY ✦✦✦

PATHS *Field tracks, woodland paths, some steep, 2 stiles*

LANDSCAPE *Farmland and hillside woodland*

SUGGESTED MAP *OS Explorer OL 27 North York Moors – Eastern*

START/FINISH *Grid reference: SE 984875*

DOG FRIENDLINESS *Can be off lead in most of woodland*

PARKING *Car park on Low Road, near road junction*

PUBLIC TOILETS *None en route*

The steep hillside of Raincliffe Woods overlooks a deep valley carved
out in the ice ages. Although mostly replanted in the 1950s and 60s,
the woods in places retain remnants of ancient oak and heather woodland
– look out for the heather and bilberry bushes beneath oak trees that will
show you where.

The Paths of the Aristocracy

The woods have long been open to the public, though in the 19th century
they were privately owned by the 1st Earl of Londesborough, and some of
the roads and tracks were named after his family – Lady Edith's Drive after
his wife and Lady Mildred's Ride after her sister. Lord Londesborough was
the grandfather of Edith, Osbert and Sacheverell Sitwell. Osbert recalled in
his autobiography *Left Hand Right Hand!* how he and Edith were taken in the
early years of the 20th century on hair-raising drives by their grandfather
in his buckboard through Raincliffe Woods. They would then walk up the
steep hillsides through columbine and honeysuckle. Unfortunately, they
often became lost, and the Earl's language was, for a time, immoderate,
until he remembered the children's presence.

Throxenby Mere

Beetle enthusiasts wax lyrical about Throxenby Mere. The last vestiges of
the huge glacial lake that formed more than 15,000 years ago, after the ice
age, it contains species of rare water beetles, and is one of the places in the
North of England to which coleopterists (beetle students to the layman)
make tracks. You will also find the distinctive pinky-purple flowers and
wide leaves of the broadleaved willowherb on its fringes.

Throughout the walk you will come upon humps and banks, depressions
and pits that show that this hillside has been a hive of human activity in the
past. As the path approaches Throxenby Mere it crosses part of a Bronze
Age dyke system, while elsewhere are medieval banks and the remains of
pits for charcoal burning. You will also pass a small quarry which was used
for local building stone.

WALK 2

The Sea Cut

In the valley below Raincliffe Woods is the Sea Cut, or North Back Drain, a flood relief channel that runs 3 miles (4.8km) from the River Derwent to Scalby Beck. Engineered in 1806 by local man, Sir George Caley, it takes excess water from the Derwent to the sea at Scalby to prevent flooding in the Vale of Pickering. Operation is by means of a sluice gate (now remotely-controlled) 825yds (755m) west of Mowthorpe Bridge near the beginning of the walk. When in operation, it restores the Derwent's link to the sea that was lost when glacial deposits blocked its original route.

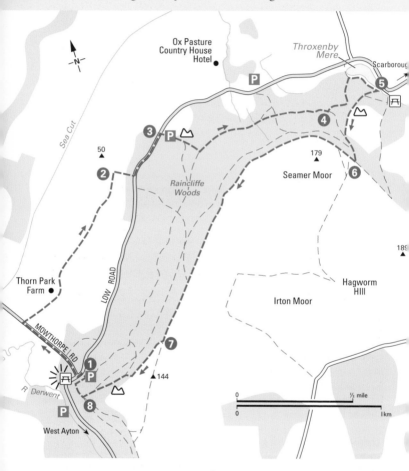

WALK 2 DIRECTIONS

1 From the car park, turn left on the road, then right at the junction. Go downhill, and after the woodland ends, pass houses on the right. Opposite a bungalow, No. 5, turn right down a track to Thorn Park Farm. Follow the track as it bends left by the farm

buildings, then right past a cottage to a metal gate. Continue to follow the track, which bends left then right, then through two gateways.

2 Just before the next gateway, turn right and walk up the field side to go through a gateway, which takes you on a short path to the road. Turn left, follow the road and continue ahead to the next car park on the right.

❸ Go up through the car park, bearing left towards a signboard, then go uphill on the path ahead. Where the main path bends right, go straight ahead, more steeply, to reach a crossing, grassy track. Turn left and follow the path. Where it forks, take the right-hand path.

❹ After 500yds (457m) look out for a faint path on the left, which immediately bends right over a drainage runnel. The path goes down into a small valley. Turn left, downhill, then follow the now-obvious path as it bends right again, past an old quarry. The path descends to reach Throxenby Mere. Turn right along the edge of the Mere – this part of the path is on boardwalks.

❺ Just before you reach a picnic place, go through a gate and immediately turn right. Follow the path which goes up steeply, ignoring all joining paths until it reaches a track at the top of the hill.

❻ Turn right and go beside a metal gate, then follow the path for a mile (1.6km), parallel with first a fence and then a wall. It passes through a gateway with a

stile by it and eventually reaches a gate with a public bridleway sign.

❼ Do not go through this gate out into fields, but turn right and continue beside the wire fence on the edge of the woodland. Where the main path swings left and another goes right, go straight ahead, steeply downhill. When the path joins another go left, down steps and along a boardwalk to meet a crossing path.

❽ Turn right and follow the path, which soon descends to the car park at the start of the walk.

Along the Coast at Robin Hood's Bay

Through fields from this obscurely-named village and back along part of the Cleveland Way.

DISTANCE 5.5 miles (8.8km) MINIMUM TIME 2hrs 30min

ASCENT/GRADIENT 466ft (142m) ▲▲▲ LEVEL OF DIFFICULTY ✦✦✦

PATHS Field and coastal paths, a little road walking, 4 stiles

LANDSCAPE Farmland and fine coastline

SUGGESTED MAP OS Explorer OL 27 North York Moors – Eastern

START/FINISH Grid reference: NZ 950055

DOG FRIENDLINESS Dogs should be on lead

PARKING Car park at top of hill into Robin Hood's Bay, by the old railway station

PUBLIC TOILETS Car park at Robin Hood's Bay

Walking the coastal path north of Robin Hood's Bay, you will soon notice how the sea is encroaching on the land. The route of the Cleveland Way, which runs in a huge clockwise arc from near Helmsley to Filey, has frequently to be redefined as sections of once-solid path slip down the cliffs into the sea. Around Robin Hood's Bay, the loss is said to be around 6 inches (15cm) every two years, with more than 200 village homes falling victim to the relentless pounding of the waves over the last two centuries.

Robin Hood's Bay

For countless holiday-makers, Robin Hood's Bay is perhaps the most picturesque of the Yorkshire Coast's fishing villages – a tumble of pantiled cottages that stagger down the narrow gully cut by the King's Beck. Narrow courtyards give access to tiny cottages, whose front doors look over their neighbours' roofs. Vertiginous stone steps link the different levels. One of the narrow ways, called The Bolts, was built in 1709, to enable local men to evade either the customs officers or the naval pressgangs – or perhaps both. Down at the shore, boats are still drawn up on the Landing, though they are more likely to be pleasure craft than working vessels.

In 1800 everyone who lived in the Bay was, supposedly, involved with smuggling. The geography of the village gave it several advantages. The approach by sea was, usually, the easiest way to the village; landward, it was defended by bleak moorland and its steep approach. And the villagers added to the ease with which they could avoid customs by linking their cellars, so that (it is said) contraband could be landed on shore and passed underground from house to house before being spirited away from the cliff top with the officers never having glimpsed it.

There was a settlement where the King's Beck reaches the coast at least as far back as the 6th century. Despite strong claims that Robin Hood was a Yorkshireman, no one has yet put forward a convincing reason why this remote fishing village should bear his name – as it has since at least the start of the 16th century. Legend is quick to step in; two of the stories say that either Robin was offered a pardon by the Abbot of Whitby if he rid the East Coast of pirates, or that, fleeing the authorities, he escaped arrest here disguised as a local sailor.

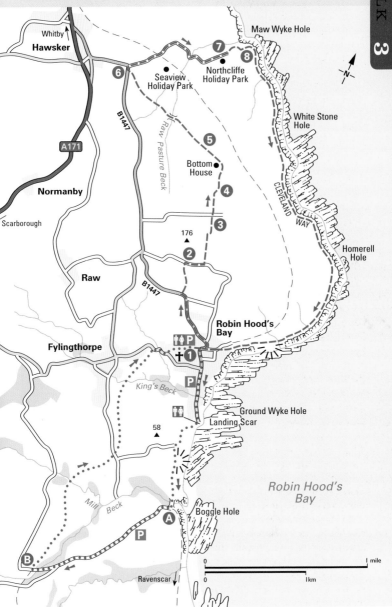

WALK 3 DIRECTIONS

1 From the car park, return via the entry road to the main road. Turn left up the hill out of the village. Just after the road bends round to the left, take a signed footpath to the right over a stile. Walk up the fields over three stiles to a metalled lane.

② Turn right. Go left through a signed metal gate. At the end of the field the path bends right to a waymarked gate in the hedge on your left. Continue down the next field with a stone wall on your left. Again, go right at the end of the field and over a stile into a green lane.

③ Cross to another waymarked stile and continue along the field edge with a wall on your right. At the field end, go over a stile on your right, then make for a waymarked gate diagonally left.

WHAT TO LOOK OUT FOR

At low tide, the bay reveals concentric arcs of rocks that are the remains of a large rock dome that has, over the millennia, been eroded by the action of the sea. The ridges are bands of hard limestone and ironstone that have eroded less quickly than the softer lias between them. Where the lias is exposed, fossil hunters search for shells and larger sea creatures.

WHERE TO EAT AND DRINK

Stoke up in Robin Hood's Bay before the walk, as there is nowhere else on the route. In the village there are several pubs and cafés, offering everything from a quick snack to a full-blown meal.

④ Walk towards the farm, through a gate and take the waymarked track through the farmyard. Continue with a stone wall on your right, through another gate and on to a track that eventually bends left to a waymarked stile.

⑤ Continue to another stile before a footbridge over a beck. Cross the bridge, then bear right across the hedge line, following the waymarker, then diagonally right towards the next waymarker and a signpost for Hawsker. Cross the stream and bear right. As the hedge to your right curves left, go through a gap on the right and over a signed stile, walking straight ahead through the field to another stile on to the main road.

⑥ Go right and right again, following the footpath sign, up the metalled lane towards the holiday parks. Pass Seaview Holiday Park,

cross the former railway track and continue along the metalled lane, which bends right, goes downhill, crosses a stream and ascends to Northcliffe Holiday Park.

⑦ Follow the Robin Hood's Bay sign right, and follow the metalled road, bending left beside a gate and down through the caravans. Just beyond them, leave the track to bear left to a waymarked path. Follow the path towards the coastline, to reach a signpost.

WHILE YOU'RE THERE

Travel south along the coast to Ravenscar, a headland where the Romans built a signal station. Alum shale, used as a fixative, was mined here in the 17th and 18th centuries. In the middle of the 19th century a new resort was begun here, then abandoned. The streets are still there, but only one row of houses was constructed.

⑧ Turn right along the Cleveland Way for 2.5 miles (4km). The footpath goes through a kissing gate and over three stiles, then through two more kissing gates. It passes through the Rocket Post Field by two more gates. Continue to follow the path as it goes past houses and ahead along a road to reach the main road. The car park is directly opposite.

Robin Hood's Bay and Boggle Hole

For a longer walk around Robin Hood's Bay, this extra loop takes you south to Boggle Hole and then back along the track of the former railway.
See map and information panel for Walk 3

DISTANCE 9.5 miles (15.3km)	**MINIMUM TIME** 4hrs		
ASCENT/GRADIENT 328ft (100m) ▲▲▲	**LEVEL OF DIFFICULTY** +++		

WALK 4 DIRECTIONS
(Walk 3 option)

After Point ❽ on Walk 3, follow the route to the main road, then turn left by the Grosvenor Hotel and walk down the steep main street of Robin Hood's Bay – notice the alleyways and steps that shoot off at all angles as you descend. At the bottom of the hill, just before you reach the shore at the Landing, turn right up Albion Road, signed 'Cleveland Way'. By Flagstaff Cottage, turn left up a flight of steps. The path ascends some boardwalk steps to reach the clifftop path. Where it turns left, through a gate, follow the Boggle Hole sign, still along the Cleveland Way.

There are good views all along the coast, with the tumbled roofs of Robin Hood's Bay behind, and the bulk of the Ravenscar headland ahead. Eventually the path descends steps to Boggle Hole, one of the classic places to find the fossilised, tightly-coiled shells of ammonites. They are the remains of dactylioceras, a marine creature, related to modern-day squid and octopus, that lived between 400 million and 60 million years ago. Ammonites vary in scale from fingernail-sized specimens to ones as large as car tyres. Locally they are known as St Hilda's Snakes, after the legend that Hilda, establishing her abbey in Whitby, found the place she had chosen infested with snakes. She used her spiritual power to decapitate them and then force them over the cliff into the sea.

Descend to cross the footbridge and ascend the other side. When you reach the metalled lane (Point Ⓐ), turn right along it, leaving the Cleveland Way. Follow the lane, going right at a fork (signed 'Fylingthorpe'), cross the stream and, part way up the hill, turn right up steps on to the former railway track at Point Ⓑ. This was the Scarborough-to-Whitby line, a 21-mile (33.8km) route opened in 1885 after 13 years' work. It closed in 1965. Follow the line, which crosses a lane and eventually reaches a main road. Turn right along the road, and after 100yds (91m) turn left, signed 'Village Hall', which comes back to the car park at Point ❶ on Walk 3.

Dracula's Whitby

Through Whitby town to see the inspiration for Bram Stoker's classic.

DISTANCE 4 miles (6.4km)	**MINIMUM TIME** 2hrs

ASCENT/GRADIENT 256ft (78m) ▲▲▲   **LEVEL OF DIFFICULTY** ✦✦✦

PATHS Coastal and field paths, then town pavements, 1 stile

LANDSCAPE Old town clustered around harbour and steep cliffs

SUGGESTED MAP OS Explorer OL 27 North York Moors – Eastern

START/FINISH Grid reference: NZ 905113

DOG FRIENDLINESS Dogs should be on lead in town

PARKING Main Abbey Car Park to east of Whitby Abbey

PUBLIC TOILETS At Whitby Abbey and (signed) in town centre

WALK 5 DIRECTIONS

Three of the most significant chapters of Bram Stoker's *Dracula*, first published in 1897, are set in Whitby. This walk takes you to some of the places where the dramatic tale is set.

From the car park, walk up the road towards the abbey. Go right at the Cleveland Way sign, through a gate at the coastline and right along the path. From this part of the coast, you can look out to sea and imagine the stormy night on which the Russian schooner *Demeter*, steered by a corpse lashed to the wheel and with its strange cargo of boxes of earth, approached Whitby harbour.

Near the National Trust Saltwick Nab sign, leave the coast along a caravan site road and walk past shops and a café. Where the Cleveland Way continues ahead, bear right through a lifting barrier, following the road. Just before a telegraph pole on the left, turn right to a waymarked stile and follow waymarks through three fields and over a stile on to the main road. Turn left down the road. Where the wall ends, take a signed path to the right, following the line of telegraph poles and passing through a kissing gate into a lane. When the lane swings right, go ahead beside a fence to a road. The town and harbour of Whitby are below: 'The River Esk runs through a deep valley which broadens out as it comes near the harbour… The houses of the old town are all red-roofed, and seem piled up one over the other anyhow,' wrote Stoker.

WHERE TO EAT AND DRINK

Whitby has all manner of pubs, restaurants and cafés, catering for every taste. If you want to sample that seaside favourite, fish and chips, the place to go is the Magpie Café near the harbour. Although you are very likely to find queues at most times, the food's certainly worth waiting for.

Cross and go down the road opposite, swinging right into The Ropery. Turn left down a cobbled slope to descend to a road. Turn right, then left just after the car park, past the Captain Cook Memorial Museum. At the end, turn left and go over the bridge, then right along the quayside. Follow the road as it bends left and then right, then turn left up a steep narrow lane, Bakehouse Yard, beside the Star Inn. At the top, turn right, up the hill. At the summit, East Crescent is to your left. Mina Murray was spending her summer in a house here with Lucy Westenra, one of Dracula's victims.

Take the steps on the right to find the Bram Stoker Memorial seat (the right-hand one on the terrace) with views of the town. On the opposite cliff are Whitby Abbey and the old parish church, where at night, in 'a narrow band of light as sharp as a sword cut', Mina saw Lucy. 'Something dark stood behind the seat where the white figure shone, and bent over it,' and she rushed headlong through the town to save her friend.

Descend through the Whalebone Arch on to the road. Turn left and go down to the harbour and back over the bridge. Just beyond, turn left down Sandgate and on to the Market Place, passing left of the Town Hall, and turning left along Church Street. As it bends right, go straight ahead to Tate Hill Pier. This is where Dracula's ship, the *Demeter*, crashed and from where 'an immense dog sprang up on

deck… and jumped from the bow…', before running off up the street.

Follow the road round into Sandside, and climb the 199 steps, up which Mina ran to save Lucy from Dracula, to the churchyard. The seat where Mina saw 'something long and black bending over the half-reclining figure' of Lucy was on the north side of the church, in the shelter of the transept. Nearby, Stoker wrote, was the grave of a suicide, where the Count spent his days in Whitby. Leave the churchyard by the iron gate at the far end, bearing left past the abbey to the car park.

WHAT TO LOOK OUT FOR

St Mary's Church, at the top of the 199 steps, has one of the oddest interiors you'll ever see. It is a 12th-century building, but it's difficult to spot this either from the outside, with its huge Georgian windows, or inside, though the semicircular chancel arch is an indication. What really hits you as you go in is the staggering number of 18th-century box pews – some complete with fireplaces – and galleries. They are crammed everywhere, painted in subtle Georgian colours and all focused on the dramatic three-decker pulpit. Even the chancel is blocked off by the elaborate Cholmley family pew, raised high on barley-sugar columns. With all this accommodation, the relatively small church could hold 2,000 people. In a vain attempt to keep those without their own pew fires warm, there is a small stove in the centre of the nave with a long chimney that disappears through the ceiling.

Early Warnings at Fylingdales and Lilla Cross

The past and the future come together on the North Yorkshire coast.

WALK 9

DISTANCE 6.75 miles (10.9km)   MINIMUM TIME 3hrs

ASCENT/GRADIENT 642ft (196m) ▲▲▲   LEVEL OF DIFFICULTY +++

PATHS Forest tracks and moorland paths, 3 stiles

LANDSCAPE Pine forest and heather moorland, with views to sea

SUGGESTED MAP OS Explorer OL 27 North York Moors – Eastern

START/FINISH Grid reference: SX 106836

DOG FRIENDLINESS Dogs should be on lead

PARKING May Beck car park, beside stream

PUBLIC TOILETS None en route

Newton House Plantation is one of the many blocks of forestry that make up the North York Moors Forest. There are more than 50,000 acres (20,250ha) of trees in the National Park, many of them, like Newton House, open for walkers. Nearly three-quarters of the timber they produce is used for sawlogs, and the rest for pulp and other products. Look out on the forest tracks for deer, and for siskins and crossbills that nest in the plantations. And keep an eye out, too, for mountain bikers, who are encouraged to use the trails.

Crossing the Moors

Unlike in most of upland Britain, the most important of the roads and tracks in the North York Moors follow the ridges between the valleys. The tracks are often marked by standing stones or crosses, many of them of great antiquity. Although many are called 'cross', most are just a base or the stump – and sometimes there's nothing to see at all. The North York Moors National Park has Ralph Cross, one of the most distinctive, as its symbol and, after the forest section, our walk passes what is left of York Cross and Ann's Cross, with the remains of John Cross to guide us on the final descent from the moors.

Lilla's Early Warning

The most impressive and most ancient of the Moor's crosses is Lilla, which commemorates a selfless deed of bravery in AD 626. King Edwin of Northumbria, whose wife Ethelburga was a Christian, was the intended victim of an assassination attempt at his court by the River Derwent near Stamford Bridge. The assassin, sent by the King of the West Saxons, lunged at Edwin with a poisoned dagger. Lilla, a Christian and one of Edwin's counsellors, leapt forward to protect the King and was killed.

Edwin had his body buried in the Bronze Age howe on the moors in sight of the sea, and had a cross, said to be the oldest Christian memorial in the North, erected in his memory. It still survives, despite a peripatetic life in the 20th century – threatened by shells from artillery ranges, it was removed to a spot by the Whitby road by the Royal Engineers in 1952. It was returned home again ten years later.

Fylingdales – Another Warning

Dominating the middle section of the walk is the improbably large sandcastle that houses the Fylingdales early warning system. It's heavily fenced and there are forbidding notices at all approaches, but from a distance it's impressive enough. It replaced the three 'Golf Balls' that became one of the sights of the Moors from the 1960s. Unlike those unexpected but satisfying spheres, the new monuments seem not yet to have been taken to visitors' hearts.

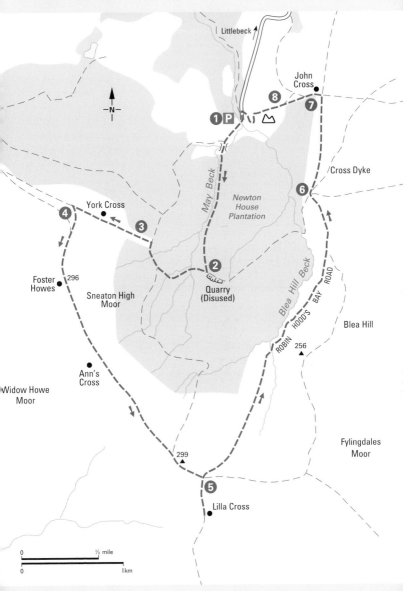

WALK 6 DIRECTIONS

1 Walk up the wide track opposite the approach road. Where the track bends round to the right, go left down a signed footpath and descend to go over a bridge and bear right to continue along the green track. Go through a kissing gate and up the valley, eventually swinging away from the stream and into the forest.

2 On reaching a forest road turn right, passing a flooded quarry on your right. At the next junction of forest roads bear right. After about 0.25 mile (400m), turn up a track to the left.

3 Go up the track, leaving forest for moorland. Continue past the base and shaft of York Cross. At a track going left, near a waymarked post, turn sharp left.

4 Walk along the track, bearing left at the Foster Howes tumuli, and continue with the fence on your right. Pass Ann's Cross to your right and 0.5 mile (800m) beyond you'll reach a T-junction. Turn right through a gate and take the track to the left.

5 When you reach a crossroads with a signpost, turn right along the track to visit Lilla Cross. Return to the crossroads, and go straight ahead, following the Robin Hood's Bay sign. Follow the path, which goes parallel with the forest edge, for 2.5 miles (4km), eventually heading for a lone tree to the right of the wood's end.

6 Bear right when you reach a post with the number 9 on it. Pass posts 8 and 7, going left when you reach a trail sign.

7 Pass post 6, (by the remains of John Cross) and go through a gate, to continue walking downhill on a track. After 50yds (46m), go left off the track and walk parallel with the woodland to a waymarked stile near the ruins of a building.

8 Go to the left of the building and ahead to another stile. Follow the obvious footpath downhill through the bracken, passing two public footpath signs, down to the road. Turn left to return to the start.

A Walk
on the Wolds

*From the hidden village of Thixendale over chalk hills
and through typical dry valleys.*

DISTANCE *4 miles (6.4km)* MINIMUM TIME *1hr 30 mins*

ASCENT/GRADIENT *459ft (140m)* ▲▲▲ LEVEL OF DIFFICULTY **✦✦**✦

PATHS *Clear tracks and field paths, 10 stiles*

LANDSCAPE *Deep, dry valleys and undulating farm land*

SUGGESTED MAP *OS Explorer 300 Howardian Hills & Malton*

START/FINISH *Grid reference: SE 842611*

DOG FRIENDLINESS *Keep dogs on lead*

PARKING *Thixendale village street near the church*

PUBLIC TOILETS *None en route*

Chalk underlies the Yorkshire Wolds. Unlike the harder rocks of the Dales and the Moors, the Wolds chalk is soft and permeable, so the landscape around here is one of rounded hills and deep dry valleys. These were formed when the meltwater from the ice age glaciers rushed with tremendous force across the chalk. Our walk is through rich farming land – indeed, these slopes have been cultivated since neolithic people cleared them and set up home here more than 5,000 years ago.

Going the Wolds Way

More than half the walk follows the Wolds Way, a 79-mile (127km) National Trail that runs from the great bridge over the Humber Estuary to Filey Brigg. At its northern end it links with the Cleveland Way and at the southern end (via the Humber Bridge) with the Viking Way to Oakham in Rutland. Less frequented than many of the other National Trails, it offers consistently fine views and a wealth of archaeological interest along its pastoral route – as well as some very welcoming pubs. For much of the walk, too, you will be following the Centenary Way, a route established by North Yorkshire County Council in 1989 to mark 100 years of local government.

Sixteen or Sigstein?

Some say that Thixendale is named from the six dry valleys that meet here. The more imaginative reckon to count 16 converging dales. Place-name dictionaries, more prosaically, derive it from a Viking called Sigstein. Whatever its origin, Thixendale is one of the most remote of the Wolds villages, approached from every direction by deep, winding dry valleys between steep chalk escarpments. It has a number of old cottages, but much of its character is due to local landowner Sir Tatton Sykes in the later part of the 19th century. As well as building estate cottages, he contributed the church, the school and the former vicarage, picturesquely designed by architect George Edmund Street. Do visit the church – the stained glass by Clayton and Bell showing the Days of Creation is great fun, especially the flamingos and the fearsome waterspout.

The Eccentric Baronet

Sir Tatton Sykes, 5th Baronet of Sledmere House, was a great church-builder and philanthropist – and an even greater eccentric. He insisted that his body needed to maintain an even temperature, and was known to stick his bare feet out of the windows of railway carriages to make sure. As he warmed up on his walks he would shed clothing, paying local boys to return it to the house. He even wore two pairs of trousers to preserve the decencies as he divested himself. Flowers were a great hate; he had the estate gardens ploughed up and told his tenants that the only kind of flowers they could grow were cauliflowers.

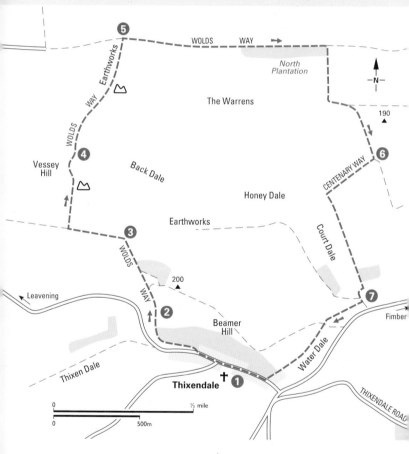

WALK 7 DIRECTIONS

❶ From the church, walk west along Thixendale's village street. Just beyond the last house on the right, go up a track, following the Wolds Way/Centenary Way sign. Cross over a ladder stile in a wire fence on your right and continue walking up the track.

❷ As you approach the top of the hill, watch out on the left for a Wolds Way sign, which takes you left along a grassy track. Go over a ladder stile then straight on along the field side to meet the track again. Continue straight ahead.

❸ At the next Wolds Way sign, go over a stile and turn left to

THIXENDALE

continue parallel to the track. At the top of the field go right by the sign. The path descends to reach a stile, descends more steeply into a dry valley to another waymarked stile, then curves to a stile by a gate.

❹ Cross the stile and follow the blue public bridleway sign to the right, winding left up the side valley. Near the top of the valley

is a deep earthwork ditch; cross over a stile and continue along the edge of the field. Where the footpath divides at an acorn waymarker go right, through the patch of woodland, on to a track by a signpost.

❺ Turn right and follow the Wolds Way sign. Follow this clear track for 0.75 mile (1.2km). At the end of the woodland on your right, look out for a signpost. Turn right here, following the Centenary Way sign to go down the edge of the field. Follow the winding footpath past two more Centenary Way signposts.

❻ At the next signpost, turn right off the track, again signed 'Centenary Way'. Walk down the field side on a grassy track. At the field end leave the track and go through a waymarked gate. The path goes left and passes along the hillside to descend to a stile beside a gate.

❼ Follow the yellow waymark straight ahead across the field. Pass over a track and continue to a sign by a stile. Go straight on, to the left of the row of trees. The path descends to the village cricket field on the valley floor. Go over a stile by a gate, on to a lane by a house. When you reach the main road, turn right, back to the start.

Mallyan Spout and Goathland's Moorland

From the popular moorland village with its television links, through woodland and over the moor.

DISTANCE 4.5 miles (7.2km)   **MINIMUM TIME** 2hrs 30min

ASCENT/GRADIENT 557ft (170m) ▲▲▲   **LEVEL OF DIFFICULTY** ✦✦✦

PATHS Rocky streamside tracks, field and moorland paths, 3 stiles

LANDSCAPE Deep, wooded valley, farmland and open moorland

SUGGESTED MAP OS Explorer OL 27 North York Moors – Eastern

START/FINISH Grid reference: NZ 827007

DOG FRIENDLINESS Dogs should be on lead

PARKING West end of Goathland village, near church

PUBLIC TOILETS Goathland village

Goathland is one of the most popular destinations for visitors to the North York Moors National Park. Its situation, around a large open common, criss-crossed by tracks and kept closely cropped by grazing sheep, has always been attractive. Today, however, many tourists are drawn to Goathland because it was used for the fictitious village of Aidensfield, setting for the popular television series *Heartbeat*. Many of the shops and businesses are now geared to visitors who want to see Aidensfield. On filming days great crowds would gather to watch the actors rehearse and go through several 'takes' as the drama unfolded.

Spouting about Mallyan

The walk begins with a visit to the 70ft (21m) Mallyan Spout waterfall into the West Beck. At this point the valley carved by the beck has a lip of much harder stone, and the little stream coming from the heather moorland above has been unable to carve its way through. In dry weather only a trickle of water may fall from the side of the gorge into the stream below – which accounts for its name of 'Spout' rather than 'Force' – but after rain it can become an impressive torrent. Take care at all times – and be aware that sometimes it may be impossible to pass the waterfall on the rocky streamside path.

Grouse and Heather

After you have crossed the ford and turned on to the moorland by Hunt House, you are likely to find yourself accompanied by the sudden flutter of red grouse as they rise from their nesting sites on the heather moorland. They feed on the young shoots of heather, so the North York Moors, which have the largest area of heather moorland south of the Scottish border, are an ideal nesting ground for them. If you visit in the late summer, the moors will be clothed in the purple of the ling heather: patches of the rarer bell heather with its flowers of a deeper purple, and the rose-pink cross-leaved heather, flower rather earlier. Sheep grazing has for centuries been the traditional way of managing the moors; the animals help keep

GOATHLAND

the heather short and encourage the new shoots. Otherwise, bracken, the pernicious opportunistic invader, will rapidly take over as much as 300 acres (121.5ha) in a single year if left unchecked. To regenerate the heather, landowners regularly use carefully-controlled burning in the early spring or the autumn when the ground is wet. The fire burns away the old 'leggy' heather stems, but does not damage the roots, nor the peat in which they grow. New growth quickly springs up to feed the young grouse.

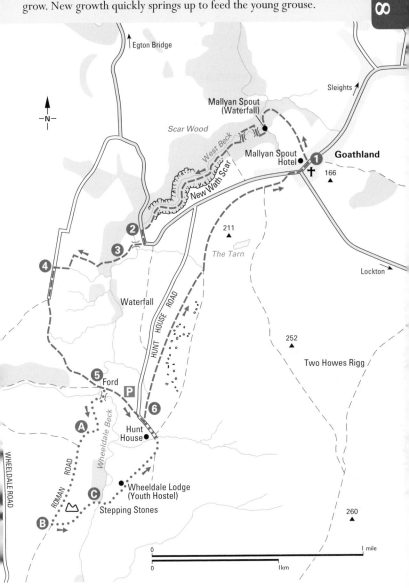

WALK 8 DIRECTIONS

❶ Opposite the church go through the kissing gate beside the Mallyan Spout Hotel, signed 'Mallyan Spout'. Follow the path to a streamside signpost and turn left. Continue past the waterfall

31

(take care after heavy rain). Follow the sometimes-difficult footpath over two footbridges, over a stile and up steps, then for another mile (1.6km) to a stile on to a road beside a bridge.

2 Turn left along the road and climb the hill. Where the road bends left, go right along a bridleway through a gate. Turn left down a path to go over a bridge, then ahead beside the buildings, through a gate and across the field.

WHAT TO LOOK OUT FOR

In the valley of the West Beck, and especially near Mallyan Spout, you will see lots of ferns. Among the sorts you might spot are the male fern, with its pale green stems, the buckler fern, which has scales with a dark central stripe and paler edges, and the hartstongue fern, with its distinctive strap-like fronds.

They are all typical of damp, humid areas, and like every fern, they are flowerless. Instead, they reproduce by means of spores – look under the leaves to find the characteristic dots that are the spore sacs or sporangia. The spores are dispersed by wind or by animals. Each young fern frond begins as a tight curl which gradually unfurls as it grows.

3 Part-way across the field, go through a waymarked gate to the right into woodland. Ascend a stony track and go through a gate, eventually turning right up the field, alongside the wall, just before

WHERE TO EAT AND DRINK

As you would expect from a popular village, there are cafés and snack bars dotted around Goathland, as well as ice cream vans on the green. The Goathland Hotel offers meals and bar snacks, and the restaurant at the Mallyan Spout Hotel has a fine reputation.

WHILE YOU'RE THERE

Take a trip on the North Yorkshire Moors Railway, which has a station in the valley below the village. Running from Pickering to Grosmont, the line was laid out by George Stephenson in 1836 for horse-drawn trains. It runs through spectacular Newtondale on its way north and ran steam trains from 1847 until it was closed in 1957. Fortunately, local enthusiasts preserved it, and it reopened in 1973. Most of its trains are steam-hauled.

you reach a facing gate as you leave the wood. Go left at the field top, through a gateway. Continue with a wall on your right and go through a waymarked gateway in the wall and up the next field, to emerge through a gate on to a metalled lane.

4 Turn left along the lane, go through a gate and follow the Roman Road sign. Go through two more gates by the farm, still following the public bridleway signs as you join a green lane. Continue through two handgates to descend to another gate and over a stile, then on until you reach a ford.

5 Cross the ford and go straight ahead along the gated track, eventually to reach a road by farm buildings. Turn right up the road and, just before a wooden garage, turn left on a green track up the hillside.

6 Bend right towards a small cairn on the ridge, then bend left, keeping below and parallel to the rocky ridge. Take a left fork by another cairn, to go slightly downhill to join a clear track. Goathland soon comes into sight. Pass a bridleway sign and descend to the road near the church, to return to the start.

Wade's Causeway

An extra loop along part of Wade's Causeway.
See map and information panel for Walk 8

DISTANCE *6.25 miles (10.1km)*   MINIMUM TIME *2hrs 30min*
ASCENT/GRADIENT *613ft (187m)* ▲▲▲   LEVEL OF DIFFICULTY ✦✦✦

WALK 9 DIRECTIONS (Walk 8 option)

At Point **5** on the main walk, cross the ford, then immediately turn right over a footbridge signed 'Roman Road'. Go right at the end of the bridge and follow the path. Go over a stile and bear left, following the waymark direction. Ascend to a wooden stile in the corner of the field and continue along the track with a wall on your left. Go through a gate, and there is a signboard to the left with details of the Roman Road, Point **A**.

Here you'll find out about the legend of Giant Wade and his wife Bell. He built the road to take his cattle to market, while she worked on Mulgrave Castle near Whitby. They had just one hammer, and they threw it the 18 miles (29km) between them as they needed it. They were a notoriously argumentative couple – the deep valley of the Hole of Horcum on the road between Whitby and Pickering is said to have been created by Wade scooping out a large handful of earth to throw at Bell. He missed, and the earth landed to form nearby Blakely Topping. Walk along the Roman Road (to the left of the modern track) and go over a stile beside a gate, following the line of the road. There is some dispute about

whether this 0.75-mile (1.2-km) stretch of ancient causeway is in fact Roman, though that seems the most likely explanation. There is also argument about its surface – is what we see now its original condition, or are these merely the foundations, with the paving of the original Roman road having been removed by locals over the centuries? Whatever the reality, you can still make out the ditches at each side of the road, the culverts still covered by stone capping in places. The road took legionaries from Malton to the signal station near Whitby, but its route has not been authenticated all the way.

About 0.25 mile (400m) beyond the gate, look for a path leading off, left, down into the valley, Point **B**. The path passes left of an anvil-shaped rock and descends steeply to stepping stones across the stream, Point **C**. Go over a stile on the other side and continue along the grassy path. Do not go along the boardwalk but continue towards the building. The path passes the building and comes out on to a track. At the signpost continue straight ahead past another farm on to a metalled lane, then turn right at the garage and back to the main walk.

Staithes and the Scenic Coast

Staithes, where Captain Cook was apprenticed, Runswick Bay and Port Mulgrave are the highlights of this splendid coastal walk.

DISTANCE 6.5 miles (10.4km)	**MINIMUM TIME** 3hrs
ASCENT/GRADIENT 436ft (133m) ▲▲▲	**LEVEL OF DIFFICULTY** +++

PATHS Field, woodland, coastal paths and tracks, 6 stiles

LANDSCAPE Farmland, woodland and fine coastline

SUGGESTED MAP OS Explorer OL 27 North York Moors – Eastern

START/FINISH Grid reference: NZ 782185

DOG FRIENDLINESS Dogs should be on lead, except in woodland

PARKING Car park above village, signed off A174

PUBLIC TOILETS Staithes

WALK 10 DIRECTIONS

From the car park, walk past the entrance to Staithes Gateway Centre and along a signed path by allotments. Turn right up the valley. At the top, turn right, then left and follow the footpath signs through the houses, eventually meeting the main road. Cross half right, go through two gates, then cross a track. Descend, bearing right at a junction of paths, go over a stile and cross the stream by the road bridge to the left, signed 'Hinderwell'. After the bridge, follow the waymark left, going over a stile and climbing steeply. Continue ahead, past a gate with a stile beside it into woodland. This part of the route is through the typical inland farming hinterland of the Yorkshire coast, with old native woodland lining the slopes of the streams that feed into Roxby Beck.

By the Oakridge Nature Reserve sign take the left fork, then go straight on, keeping along the narrow ridge. Just before a field, turn left then right, over a stile and along the field-edge. At a crossing path, turn left back into the woods. Descend steps, cross a footbridge and go uphill over two stiles. Cross the field, then turn right after the gate and stile and go along a track, which eventually bends left and becomes a metalled road through houses.

At the main road by a garage turn right, and then turn left along a path before the last bungalow. Go over a stile, through the field and over another stile on to a road. Turn right along the lane-side footpath to Runswick Bay. To see the view, go straight to the cliff top. The pretty village is at the foot of the steep cliffs, and has been there since at least the 13th century. In

WHERE TO EAT AND DRINK

Staithes has quite a number of eating places, as you'd expect from somewhere on the Captain Cook Trail. Fine dining is on offer at The Endeavour on the main street; The Cod and Lobster, near the harbour, does meals and snacks, while Sea Drift, by the harbour, does splendid sandwiches.

STAITHES

the 19th century the village briefly had a blast furnace, but is now renowned for its fine sandy beach.

The walk continues on a signed footpath along the right side of the Runswick Bay Hotel. Go through a kissing gate and along the edge of a field to a stile to reach the coast. Turn left and walk along the Cleveland Way for a mile (1.6km) to a kissing gate near Port Mulgrave. Bend left after it round the top of the valley to another gate. From 1865 Port Mulgrave was an ironstone port. Its 3.5-acre (1.4ha) harbour cost the Mulgrave Ironstone Company £45,000 to build. Trucks ran along a gantry above the pier and tipped their load into bunkers – there was a tunnel under the cliffs through which the railway line ran. The harbour remained in good condition until 1934, when the

machinery was broken up and sold for scrap. During World War Two, the breakwater was blown up so it couldn't be used by an invader.

Continue along the coast road, which soon becomes a track. Go along the coast, through a gate and descend towards Staithes. Go through two gates and into a fenced lane, which becomes a metalled lane by a farm. The path descends by a wall down into the village.

Clustered around the harbour and along the banks of the Roxby Beck, Staithes is one of the most attractive of the East Coast villages. Its narrow streets, lined with cottages, climb steeply up the hillside. Look out for the occasional wearer of the traditional white cotton Staithes bonnet, originally worn by the women to protect their heads as they carried baskets of mussels from the beach. It was in Staithes that young James Cook – the future Captain Cook – was apprenticed to William Sanderson's grocers' merchants in the main street. The Heritage Centre has a reconstruction of the street in his time.

To return to the car park, walk up the main street.

WHAT TO LOOK OUT FOR

Staithes harbour is protected by the shaley cliff of Cowbar Nab, and you are likely to see a number of small, colourfully-painted boats bobbing in the water or leaning in the mud if the tide is out. These are cobles (pronounced cobbles), the characteristic small fishing boats of the east coast. Inspired, it is said, by Viking boats, they are clinker-built – with the planks overlapping downwards – and are specially designed for launching from a beach. A guide of the 19th century said of the local men, 'During the winter and spring seasons they go out to sea in small flat bottomed boats, called Cobles, each carrying three men, and so constructed as to live in very tempestuous weather; in summer they go out in large boats, of from ten to twenty tons burden, called 'Five Men Cobles', they generally sail on Monday, and, if the weather permit, continue at sea the whole week.'

Overleaf: Staithes village from Cowbar Nab (Walk 10)

A Lastingham Round

*From the ancient site of St Cedd's monastery
to the attractive village of Hutton-le-Hole.*

DISTANCE 4.5 miles (7.2km)   **MINIMUM TIME** 2hrs

ASCENT/GRADIENT 463ft (141m) ▲▲▲   **LEVEL OF DIFFICULTY** ✦✦✦

PATHS Farm tracks and field paths, 2 stiles

LANDSCAPE Moorland and woodland, with views

SUGGESTED MAP OS Explorer OL 26 North York Moors – Western

START/FINISH Grid reference: SE 729905

DOG FRIENDLINESS Dogs should be on lead

PARKING Village street in Lastingham. Alternative parking in car park at north end of Hutton-le-Hole

PUBLIC TOILETS Hutton-le-Hole

'In high and isolated hills, more fitted as a place of robbers and the haunt of wild animals than somewhere fit for men to live.'

So wrote the 8th-century historian Bede about Lastingham, which he had visited. This was where St Cedd, Bishop of the East Saxons and once a monk from Lindisfarne, founded his monastery in AD 654, and where he died in AD 664. Although nothing survives of his church, Lastingham remains a holy place, not least in the ancient and impressive crypt beneath the Norman church. This was built in 1078, when the monastery was refounded after destruction in Danish raids in the 9th century.

Court in Spaunton

Leaving Lastingham, the walk quickly reaches the single village street of Spaunton. Lined with cottages and farmhouses from the 17th century onwards, it seems typical of many villages on the North York Moors. But Spaunton has hidden secrets; the fields surrounding it are set out on a Roman pattern, and at the beginning of the 19th century, a Roman burial was found near the village. Excavations, some 60 years later, also unearthed the foundations of a very large medieval hall, which indicated that Spaunton was once a large and important village, owned by St Mary's Abbey in York. When the estate was sold in the 16th century, the new landowners constituted a special court for the manor, grandly called the Court Leet and Court Baron with View of Frankpledge, which still meets to deal with the rights of those who can graze animals on the commons.

Hutton-le-Hole and the Quakers

Reckoned by many people to be one of the prettiest of North Yorkshire's villages, Hutton-le-Hole clusters around an irregular green and along the banks of the Hutton Beck. The village has an old Meeting House and a long association with the Society of Friends. One Quaker inhabitant, John Richard, was a friend of William Penn, founder of Pennsylvania. He spent much time

LASTINGHAM

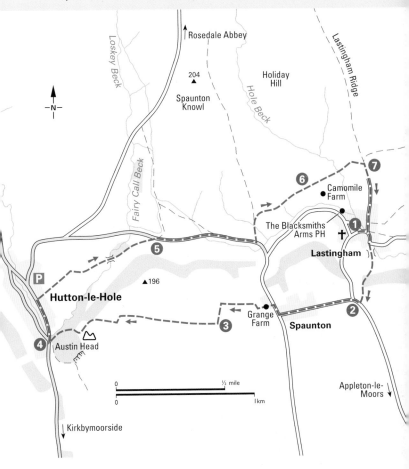

preaching in America; it is said he rode more than 3,726 miles (5,995km) and acted as a mediator between the white settlers and the Native Americans. He finally retired to the village, where he died in 1753.

The Millennium Stone

Near the end of the walk you'll come across a new local landmark. Marking the year 2000, the people of Lastingham have placed a boulder carved with a cross on the hillside above the village. On it are two dates – AD 2000 and AD 654, the year in which St Cedd founded the original Lastingham monastery.

WALK 11 DIRECTIONS

1 Begin by The Green and follow signs to Cropton, Pickering and Rosedale, past the red telephone box. Where the road swings left, go right to wind over a small bridge and beside a stream. Ascend to a footpath sign, and go right, uphill, through a gate and through woodland to a handgate on to a road. Turn right, signed 'Spaunton'.

2 Follow the road through Spaunton, and bend right at the end of the village, then turn left by the public footpath sign over the cattle grid into the farmyard. The waymarked track curves through the farm to reach another footpath signpost, where the track bends left. After 100yds (91m), at a barn, the track bends left again.

❸ After about 200yds (183m), follow a public footpath sign right and walk on to follow another sign as the track bends left. After 100yds (91m), take a footpath to the right, down the hill into woodland. Follow the track as it bends left, then go right, following the waymarks, down a steep grassy path into the valley. Descend to a gate beside a stream, and on to the road through Hutton-le-Hole.

❹ Turn right up the main street and then right again at a footpath signpost opposite the Village Hall. Follow the waymarked route along the field-edges and through five waymarked gates to a kissing gate before a footbridge. Follow the path through woodland to a gate and follow the grassy track to the road.

WHILE YOU'RE THERE

If you're a real ale enthusiast, Cropton Brewery, 1.5 miles (2.4km) east of Lastingham, is a place to head for. It can brew up to 60 barrels a week, and produces a range of beers with evocative names such as Monkmans Slaughter and Honey Gold, made with local honey. The Brewery and visitor centre are open daily during the season, and by arrangement in the winter. Sample the beer at The New Inn in Cropton.

❺ Turn right and follow the road for 0.5 mile (800m). Turn left at a footpath sign just before the road descends to a stone bridge. Continue on the grassy path, going over a stile, and follow the track towards a farm.

WHERE TO EAT AND DRINK

There is a range of cafés, tea rooms, restaurants and pubs in Hutton-le-Hole – the Barn Tea Rooms and The Crown Hotel are recommended. In Lastingham, The Blacksmith's Arms is a traditional village pub, while the excellent Lastingham Grange offers dinner and light lunches, as well as a full Sunday lunch, but is closed from mid-November to March.

❻ Follow the waymarked posts, bending left alongside the wall beside a clump of trees and descending into a valley. Cross over the stream and follow the wall on your right-hand side uphill. You will reach a bench and then a carved stone with a cross and a three-pointed sign nearby.

❼ Take none of the directions indicated by the sign, but turn right, downhill through a gate and on to the metalled road. Follow the road downhill back into the village of Lastingham.

WHAT TO LOOK OUT FOR

There is a full range of activities at the Ryedale Folk Museum in Hutton-le-Hole, where old structures from around the North York Moors have been reconstructed as a hamlet. As well as an authentic Elizabethan manor house with a massive oak cruck frame, farm buildings, cottages and traditional long houses, you can see an early photographer's studio, a medieval glass kiln and a variety of agricultural tools and transport. There's also a fire engine and a hearse. Maypole dancing, rare breeds days and quilting are just some of the activities that take place during the year and you may catch the historic farm machinery working, or have the chance to try your hand at some of the almost-forgotten crafts.

Opposite: Sheep graze on Hutton-le-Hole village green next to Hutton Beck (Walk 11)

Glorious Castle Howard

A walk around the well-ordered estates of one of the country's most famous stately homes

DISTANCE 5.25 miles (8.4km)	**MINIMUM TIME** 2hrs
ASCENT/GRADIENT 256ft (78m) ▲▲▲	**LEVEL OF DIFFICULTY** ✦✦✦

PATHS Field paths and estate roads, no stiles

LANDSCAPE Estate landscape and farmland

SUGGESTED MAP OS Explorer 300 Howardian Hills & Malton

START/FINISH Grid reference: SE 708710

DOG FRIENDLINESS Dogs should be on lead for much of walk

PARKING Roadside car park near lake north-west of Castle Howard, near crossroads

PUBLIC TOILETS None en route (toilets at Castle Howard)

One of the greatest of England's stately homes, Castle Howard was designed in 1699 by John Vanbrugh for Charles Howard, 3rd Earl of Carlisle. Vanbrugh was not an architect; he made his reputation first as a soldier, then as a playwright, so he was an odd choice. Nevertheless, he rose to the task in superb style. The north front, which we see from the first part of the walk, is hugely dramatic, with its giant columns, curving wings and crowning dome. One early visitor, Horace Walpole, wrote, 'I have seen gigantic palaces before, but never a sublime one.'

'A Perfect Landskip'

Everyone who visits Castle Howard will soon realise that this great house is set in a landscape that has been carefully manipulated as a setting for the house. The impressive 3.75-mile (6km) long, ruler-straight avenue that passes through the fortified Carrmire Gate and the Pyramid Gate, is only the start. Virtually everything of the estate you will see on the walk has been altered – hills rounded or levelled, rivers re-routed and dammed, lakes dug. All this was to create what the 18th-century writers called 'a perfect landskip', based on Italian paintings and dotted with classical buildings.

Pyramid and Mausoleum

There are three pyramids at Castle Howard – one of them is over the Pyramid Gate, one is in Pretty Wood and the third, the 'Great' Pyramid, is a landmark on the second part of this walk. Surrounded by four stone lanterns this pyramid (not open to the public) holds a monster bust of the 3rd Earl's great-great-grandfather. To the right as you approach the ornamental bridge over the New River, created in the 1740s, is the splendid Mausoleum, designed by Nicholas Hawksmoor. It is the final resting place for many generations of the Howard family, including Lord Howard of Henderskelfe, a former Chairman of the BBC. From the ornamental bridge there are fine views of the south façade of the house itself and its distinctive gilded dome.

CASTLE HOWARD

Beyond the bridge is the Temple of the Four Winds, each portico inviting fresh breezes from the cardinal points of the compass. This little building by Vanbrugh is at the end of a terraced walk from the house. It is said that this walk was originally the main street of the village of Henderskelfe, swept away by the 3rd Earl and his architect in their grandiose scheme. Plans were drawn up for a new village nearby, but, somehow, it was never built. Beyond, notice the garden wall; the ground is higher on the house side, and is retained by a solid, rustic wall with a ditch in front of it – an early ha-ha, which allowed uninterrupted views of the countryside without the inconvenience of sheep in the drawing room.

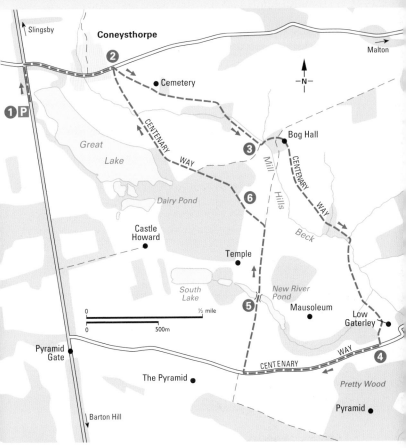

WALK 12 DIRECTIONS

❶ From the roadside car park, turn left to reach the crossroads and then turn right towards Coneysthorpe. Walk right through the attractive village, and, just beyond the 'Slow' road marking, go right through a tall white gate in a wall.

❷ Go half left, following the Bog Hall sign. Cross the track and head towards the further telegraph pole, passing the cemetery on your left. Go through a gate, then bend right along the edge of a field and, when you reach the double gate, turn right again along the edge of the wood. Continue along the track to reach a bridge.

43

CASTLE HOWARD

3 Do not cross the bridge, but turn left along the track, following it as it bends right through the farm buildings, following the Welburn and CW signs. The track passes a wood and winds over a bridge. At the next farm buildings follow the Centenary Way sign to the right.

4 At the T-junction, turn right along the metalled lane. The Pyramid comes into view. As you near the Pyramid, you will reach a staggered crossroads. Turn right here, signed 'Coneysthorpe', and descend to the bridge over the dammed stream, with the Mausoleum on the right and Castle Howard on the left.

5 Cross the bridge, go through the gate then bear left, with the Temple of the Four Winds on

your left. The path goes over the ridge, then turns left to the park wall. Follow the wall as it bends left and go though a kissing gate beside a white gate and continue along the track.

6 After about 50yds (46m), just beyond a gate on your left, go left off the track down a grassy path. Follow this, keeping parallel to the estate wall to another track. Cross the track, then bear half left to reach another track. Turn right here and follow this track back to the tall white gate in Coneysthorpe. Turn left through the gate, and retrace your route back to the car park.

Opposite: The Mausoleum of 1742 and bridge in the grounds of Castle Howard (Walk 12)

The Iron Valley of Rosedale

*Reminders of former industry are all around you
on this route near Rosedale Abbey.*

DISTANCE *3.5 miles (5.7km)*   MINIMUM TIME *1hr 30min*

ASCENT/GRADIENT *558ft (170m)* ▲▲▲   LEVEL OF DIFFICULTY ✦✦✦

PATHS *Mostly field paths and tracks, 7 stiles*

LANDSCAPE *Quiet valley and hillside farmland, with reminders
of the iron industry*

SUGGESTED MAP *OS Explorer OL 26 North York Moors – Western*

START/FINISH *Grid reference: SE 717970*

DOG FRIENDLINESS *Dogs should be on lead*

PARKING *Roadside parking near road junction north-east of Rosedale Abbey,
near Sycamore Farm sign*

PUBLIC TOILETS *None en route*

Rosedale is a quiet and peaceful valley that pushes north-west into the heart of the North York Moors. The village of Rosedale Abbey gets its name from the former Cistercian nunnery, founded in 1158 and closed in 1536. The nuns are reputed to have introduced sheep farming to the North York Moors. Only an angle of a wall remains, containing a broken stairway. Rosedale may be peaceful today, but little more than 100 years ago the village had a population ten times its present size after the discovery of ironstone in the hills in the mid-1850s led to commercial exploitation. As one of the villagers wrote in 1869, 'The ground is hollow for many a mile underground… It's like a little city now but is a regular slaughter place. Both men and horses are getting killed and lamed every day.'

The East Mines

The dramatic remains of the Rosedale East Mines, which opened in 1865, can be seen during much of the walk. They are a testament to the size of the mining operations. The long range of huge arches is the remains of the calcining kilns, where the ironstone was roasted to eliminate impurities and reduce its weight. They operated until 1879, when the owner, the Rosedale and Ferryhill Mining Company, collapsed, but resumed in 1881. The West Mines across the valley had stopped work by 1890, but the East Mines struggled on, burdened by rising costs, until the General Strike of 1926 killed them off.

The Iron Way

The iron ore from Rosedale was taken by rail over the moorland to Ingleby, where it was lowered down the northern edge of the moors by tramway on the 1-in-5 gradient Ingleby Incline. The line had reached Rosedale in 1861, and the branch to the East Mines was opened in 1865. As many as 15 loaded wagons at a time were steam hauled round the top of Rosedale. The line closed in September 1928, and the last load was hauled down Ingleby Incline in June 1929. The track bed is now open to walkers.

ROSEDALE ABBEY

The Vanished Chimney

For more than a century the village of Rosedale Abbey was dominated by an industrial chimney, more than 100ft (30m) tall. One of the steepest public roads in the country went past it to reach the heights of Spaunton Moor. The road is still there, but the chimney was demolished in 1972, a victim of the inability to raise the £6,000 needed to preserve it.

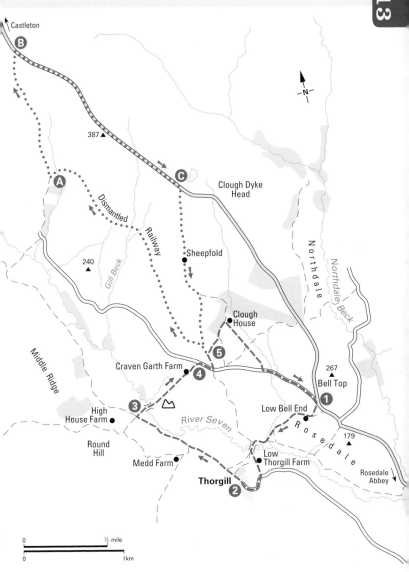

WALK 13 DIRECTIONS

❶ From the parking place take the lane downhill by the Sycamore Farm sign. It bends right. Follow the waymarkers to turn right through Low Bell End Farm gateway. Follow the track through two gates and continue downhill. Near a gate on the left the track

47

WALK 13

bends right, following the stream. After going through another gateway, bend left towards the stream to cross a footbridge with stiles at each end. Follow the waymarked footpath half left, uphill, towards the farm buildings. The route passes through the buildings and on to a farm track. Follow the track uphill, forking right to reach a lane. Turn right.

② Continue up the metalled lane, which takes you through the hamlet of Thorgill. Just beyond the buildings the metalled lane soon becomes a track. Follow the track for 0.75 mile (1.2 km), going through a wooden gate near Medd Farm and continuing downhill. Pass a small caravan site called Seven Side and begin to rise again. Almost opposite another farmhouse – High House Farm – on the left, go right over a waymarked wooden stile beside a gate.

WHILE YOU'RE THERE
Take the road north from Rosedale Abbey to Rosedale Head, where you will find Young Ralph Cross, symbol of the North York Moors National Park. A little way to the west is Old Ralph. Young Ralph is 18th century, replacing one on the site from at least 1200. Old Ralph, on the highest part of Blakey Ridge, is possibly 11th century.

③ Walk down the slope beside the fence and pass over the River Seven on a gated footbridge. At the end, turn left to go uphill – a short but steep slope. At the top, the path

WHERE TO EAT AND DRINK
The Milburn Arms Hotel in Rosedale Abbey offers high-class dining in its Priory Restaurant as well as meals in the beamed bar. The Abbey Tea Rooms provides light lunches and cream teas daily from Easter to November – weekends only in winter.

goes above the stream, generally parallel with it. Continue through a gate into the field and walk ahead. Go through another gate and continue up the field with a fence on your left. Go through a metal gate into the yard of Craven Garth Farm. Go through another gateway and pass between the cluster of buildings to reach a metalled country lane at a T-junction.

④ Turn right and follow the lane; just before reaching the row of former ironworkers' cottages, look for the Rosedale parish notice board on the left. Turn up the track beside it. A little way up the track, before reaching the farm, look for a gate across a track to Clough House.

⑤ Go over the stile beside the gate and follow the track downhill towards the wood. The track bends right just before Clough House, then bends left to pass the front of the house. Opposite the building, go through a waymarked gate on the right and walk down the field towards houses. Leave the field by a gate, and follow the track to the road. Turn left and follow the road back to the car parking place.

WHAT TO LOOK OUT FOR
Looming over Thorgill is the bulk of Blakey Rigg, one of the most prominent of the Moors' heights, which divides Rosedale and Farndale. The Hutton-le-Hole to Castleton road follows the ridge's top for most of its length, providing superb views. The Rigg is also known as a landmark on the Lyke Wake Walk across the Moors, celebrated in the Lyke Wake Dirge starting 'This aye night', set by Benjamin Britten. The walk follows the route that corpses were taken for burial.

Along the Railway to Rosedale East Mines

Those who want to explore Rosedale's ironworking heritage further can take this loop, that starts by following the old railway line.
See map and information panel for Walk 13

| DISTANCE **8 miles (12.9km)** | MINIMUM TIME **3hrs 15min** |
| ASCENT/GRADIENT **492ft (150m)** ▲▲▲ | LEVEL OF DIFFICULTY ✦✦✦ |

WALK 14 DIRECTIONS (Walk 13 option)

At Point ❺ on the main walk, don't go over the stile signed 'Clough House', but instead continue ahead up the lane. Pass the farmhouse and continue ahead up the track.

There is a National Park information board giving details of the railway route and the mines a little way along. Just beyond the information board, go through a wooden gate and follow the path ahead, to pass round the ruined buildings. Turn right along the track of the dismantled railway, which opened in 1865 and closed in 1928.

There are still reminders of the working days of the railway all the way along here, including a small platelayers' hut. Follow the old track bed for 1.5 miles (2.4km). You will pass the remains of the Rosedale East Mines calcining kilns. Just after the track passes over a high embankment with woodland to the left, turn right uphill, to reach Point ❹. There is a deep gill to the right and a stream on the left.

Follow the path uphill on to the plateau. It eventually passes near one of the many estate boundary markers of the moors and will bring you to the metalled road by a public bridleway sign, Point ❸.

Turn right and follow the minor road for about 1 mile (1.6km) across the almost flat moorland plateau. Ignore sign to Rosedale on the right and continue to the next bridleway sign (Point ❻) just beyond some old quarry workings. Follow the very faint path half left through the heather, passing to the right of another disused quarry, and eventually going parallel with a wall to reach the ruins of a sheepfold.

The track becomes more distinct now; follow it downhill towards the valley. When it bends to a wire fence, walk with the fence on your left to return to the gate by the National Park information board.

Turn left through the gate, and continue past the farm buildings. Then take the stile on the left beside the gate signposted 'Clough House'. You rejoin the main route back at Point ❺ to complete the walk.

49

Princes and Poets at Sheriff Hutton

The ruined castle of the Nevilles provides the focus for this walk on the edge of the Vale of York.

DISTANCE 6 miles (9.7km)   **MINIMUM TIME** 2hrs 30min

ASCENT/GRADIENT 147ft (45m) ▲▲▲   **LEVEL OF DIFFICULTY** ✦✦✦

PATHS Field paths and tracks, a little road walking, 9 stiles

LANDSCAPE Undulating farmland, with the castle set on a ridge

SUGGESTED MAP OS Explorer 300 Howardian Hills & Malton

START/FINISH Grid reference: SE 654664

DOG FRIENDLINESS Dogs should be kept on lead

PARKING Roadside parking in village

PUBLIC TOILETS Sheriff Hutton

WALK 15 DIRECTIONS

From the crossroads – The Square – in the village centre, walk down the hill. Where the road bends right, turn left over a stile, signed 'Centenary Way and Ebor Way' and walk by a playground. Walk down the field, keeping the hedge on your right. You can clearly see Sheriff Hutton Castle to your left. Begun in 1382 by the Neville family, it originally had four huge corner towers, though only one remains to any great height. It was one of the power bases for the Earl of Warwick, known as the Kingmaker, whose daughter, Anne, married Richard III. Elizabeth of York, later queen to Henry VII, was imprisoned here until her future husband won the Battle of

Bosworth in 1485. Sheriff Hutton Castle was subsequently owned by the Earl of Surrey, who employed the poet John Skelton to provide flattering verses for his household. Skelton's *Garlande of Laurell* was written here at Christmas in 1522.

Just past the cricket score box, go over a waymarked stile on your right, and continue along the cricket field edge. Go over another stile and straight on. At the end of the field, go over a bridge with stiles at each end and ahead. At the metalled track, turn left and continue through two gateways. When you see a stile to your left, before reaching woodland, go half right across the field, keeping left of the telegraph pole. Go over a stile in the crossing wire fence and go half right. In the top corner, where the field narrows, go over a footbridge between two waymarked stiles. Turn left after the second, over a wire fence, and follow the hedge, bending at the end to a gated footbridge in a crossing hedge. After the second gate, go half right across the field between humps in the ground,

---

WHERE TO EAT AND DRINK

The Highwayman Inn in The Square offers pub food in the bar and restaurant (not Mondays). It has a beer garden and welcomes children. The Castle Inn serves lunchtime and early evening meals every day except Wednesday.

the distance. The city's skyline has been kept deliberately low to allow this huge building to make its full impact on the landscape.

After 0.5 mile (800m), take the second turn right. Walk beside the farm buildings to go through two waymarked gates, beside a pond and through another gate. Cross two fields to a gate in the crossing hedge. Continue towards the farm buildings, passing through another gate. Opposite the end of the farm buildings, turn left to a stile in a crossing fence. Continue down the field towards the castle, going over a stile and footbridge. Ascend the next field, turn right at the top and bear left up a hedged lane to enter the churchyard through a gate. In the church, which was first built in the 11th century, is an alabaster figure that is said to be part of a monument to Edward, Prince of Wales, son of Richard III. He died at Middleham Castle in 1485 and his mother is supposed to have met his funeral procession here.

Leave the churchyard by another gate on to the road and turn left back to The Square.

keeping left of the telegraph poles. These are the remains of the deserted village of East Lilling. You can make out the rectangular platforms on which the houses were built, amidst the typical ridge and furrow of early ploughing.

Cross a stream and continue to a stile, and on in the same direction, to go over a boardwalk. After another gateway with a bridge after it, bend right to go on to a road at a gate. Turn left, and left again at the crossroads, signed 'Bulmer'. About 0.25 mile (400m) beyond Thornton Grange Farm, go left up a concrete track towards Lodge Farm. Look south from the track to see York Minster in

Remote Cockayne and Rudland Rigg

A walk in Bransdale from the remote hamlet of Cockayne and along an ancient moorland track.

DISTANCE *4 miles (6.4km)*   MINIMUM TIME *2hrs*

ASCENT/GRADIENT *754ft (230m)* ▲▲▲   LEVEL OF DIFFICULTY ✦✦✦

PATHS *Field paths and moorland tracks, a little road walking, 2 stiles*

LANDSCAPE *Farmland and heather moorland*

SUGGESTED MAP *OS Explorer OL 26 North York Moors – Western*

START/FINISH *Grid reference: SE 620985*

DOG FRIENDLINESS *On lead in farmland*

PARKING *Roadside parking near cattle grid at T-junction in Cockayne*

PUBLIC TOILETS *None en route*

The hamlet of Cockayne is tucked away at the end of Bransdale, one of the most remote of the valleys of the North York Moors. Here the road loops back into the lower moors, and walking country lies ahead. Its remoteness may be the origin of its name; the 'Land of Cockayne' was a distant and mythical place, of idleness and luxury, popular in medieval literature. Pleasant though Cockayne may be in good weather, any idleness in winter is no doubt enforced by the results of its isolation.

The Literary Mill

After leaving Cockayne, the first substantial building you will come to is Bransdale Mill. Here the infant Hodge Beck has been dammed into a series of pools to feed the millwheel. They may date back as far as the 13th century, when Bransdale Mill is first recorded. The current buildings are, however, from 600 years later, when the mill was rebuilt, as the inscription says, by local landowner William Strickland. His son Emmanuel was responsible for the inscriptions that adorn the buildings, in Latin, Greek and Hebrew. Emmanuel was vicar of Ingleby Greenhow, 6.25 miles (10.1km) to the north, over the hills.

Making Tracks

After the climb from the traditional farm buildings at Spout House, the walk takes you on some of the many tracks that cross the high moorland. As you pass the grouse butts you are on an ancient route that traverses the ridge from Farndale (famous for its wild daffodils) into Bransdale. Soon you will turn left along Westside Road. Like most of the main routes in the North York Moors, it follows the summit of the ridge; this one is Rudland Rigg. Westside Road is one of the longest (and straightest) in the National Park, running 34.25 miles (55km) north from Kirkbymoorside to leave the northern edge of the Moors near Kildale. Along its route you will find old stone waymarks and boundary stones. As you leave the track along the ridge, you are rewarded with a view back down into Bransdale.

Acorns Restore

Much of the north end of the valley is owned by the National Trust, and Bransdale Mill, passed at the beginning of the walk, is a centre for volunteers on the Trust's Acorn Projects – indeed, it was they who restored the buildings. Bransdale has also been suggested as the home of Robin Hood (fairly handy for his Bay, perhaps!), but this is probably only the result of confusion with Barnsdale Forest, more than 31.5 miles (50km) to the south, which is a rather more likely area for the outlaw's home.

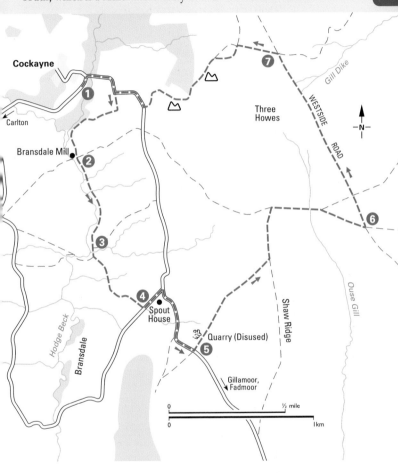

WALK 16 DIRECTIONS

❶ From your parking place in Cockayne, cross the cattle grid and bend right towards Kirkbymoorside. Follow the road uphill and, as it bends sharp left, go through a gate beside a sign 'Bransdale Basecamp' and follow the track down the hill to a gate. Continue along the track.

❷ At the signpost by the crossroads of tracks next to Bransdale Mill carry straight on, continuing parallel with the stream on your right. Go through two gates, following the side of the stream. Climb over a slight ridge to reach another gate. Continue with a wire fence on your right, keeping on the ridge, then descend to a waymarked gate.

WHERE TO EAT AND DRINK

The isolation of Cockayne means there are no pubs or tea rooms along the walk. In Gillamoor, The Royal Oak Inn offers home cooking, Sunday lunches and some excellent Yorkshire beers, while nearby in Fadmoor, the Plough Inn has a traditional atmosphere and excellent food.

❸ Cross the stream and continue ahead. At the top of a rise, go half left across the field, making for a corner of the wall. Go through three waymarked field gates and follow the grassy track along the field-edge to another waymarked gate. At the top of the field go over a stile beside a wooden gate on to a lane.

❹ Turn left. Pass the farm buildings to a road junction and turn right. Follow the road uphill for 0.25 mile (400m). At a bridleway signpost turn left on to the moorland.

❺ Follow the path through the heather to a track, where you turn left. Follow the track to reach a metal barrier. Turn right at the junction just beyond and follow the track to a crossroads.

WHAT TO LOOK OUT FOR

The rough-legged buzzard has sometimes been seen in Bransdale – though its appearance can't be guaranteed. The feathers on its legs have led to its name, and mean it can be distinguished from its smooth-legged brothers, the common and the honey buzzard. In Britain they can be found in Scotland and eastern England, where they come in the winter from their arctic breeding grounds in northern Scandinavia – they have not been known to breed here. Their main food is small mammals, though they are not above feeding off dead farm animals. If they're around, you are likely to see them in the air, though they have occasionally been spotted on low fences and gateposts, watching keen-eyed for their prey.

WHILE YOU'RE THERE

If you're visiting in spring, take a trip over the ridge into Farndale. Along the banks of the River Dove, wild daffodils flower in great drifts of yellow, drawing many visitors to follow the Daffodil Trail. The bulbs may have been planted by monks in the Middle Ages. There's a Farndale Daffodil Shuttle Bus service along the dale, which you should use to prevent congestion.

❻ Turn left and follow the gravel track for 0.75 mile (1.2km), past a boundary stone and the Three Howes tumuli. Where the gravel track is crossed by a grass track, turn left, following the bridleway mark on the post.

❼ Follow the track downhill. It passes the end of a wood and continues to wind downhill. Go through a wooden gate and then bend left along the field-edge to a stile beside a gate on to the lane. Turn right and follow the road back to the starting point.

Opposite: Daffodils growing in Farndale (Walk 16)

Hidden York

Through streets and alleys of the historic walled city.

DISTANCE *3.25 miles (5.3km)*   MINIMUM TIME *1hr 30min*

ASCENT/GRADIENT *82ft (25m)* ▲▲▲   LEVEL OF DIFFICULTY ✦✦✦

PATHS *City pavements*

LANDSCAPE *Historic city*

SUGGESTED MAP *AA Street by Street York Page 2 C3*

START/FINISH *Grid reference: SE 598523*

DOG FRIENDLINESS *City streets, so dogs on lead*

PARKING *Marygate Car Park, off Bootham*

PUBLIC TOILETS *Museum Gardens and Bootham Bar*

St Olave's Church, at the start of the walk, was founded in 1055 by Siward, Earl of Northumbria and heavily repaired after it was used as a gun platform in 1644 during the Civil War Siege of York. Further along, past the library, look right, as you ascend the steps, to the Anglian Tower. Built on the Roman ramparts during the time the Anglians ruled York (from the 6th century), this small building is now surrounded by the exposed layers of successive York defensive walls.

Abbot and Archbishop

The King's Manor, on your left as you go towards Exhibition Square, was the house of the Abbot of St Mary's, and was appropriated by the King in 1539. The residence of the President of the Council of the North from 1561 to 1641, it was apartments until 1833 and then a school. Since 1963 it has been leased to York University. The Minster Library, approached through Dean's Park, north of the Minster, is the only remaining substantial part of the palace of the Archbishops of York. Built about 1230 as the palace's chapel, it became the library in the 19th century.

Vicars and Nonconformists

Bedern, off Goodramgate, was where the Vicars Choral of the Minster lived. They sang the Minster services, and had their own Chapel and Hall (both of which you will pass) as well as a wooden walkway to the Minster precincts to avoid the undesirables who inhabited the area. On St Saviourgate is the red-brick Unitarian Chapel. Designed in the shape of an equal-armed cross with a little tower, it was built for the Presbyterians in 1692. Lady Peckitt's Yard is beside the spectacular half-timbered Herbert House of about 1620. As you turn into Fossgate, notice Macdonald's furniture shop opposite. This was the Electric Theatre, York's first cinema, built in 1911. After passing Clifford's Tower and reaching Castlegate, visit Fairfax House, a fine town house of the 1740s with its interiors beautifully restored in the 1980s after it, too, was used as a cinema for many years. On King's Staith, once the main wharf for the city, is the 17th-century King's Arms Inn, which has the distinction of being Britain's most flooded pub. Ouse Bridge was, for centuries, the only crossing place linking the two banks of the river. This 19th-century bridge replaced two earlier ones: the Elizabethan bridge had houses on it. Holy Trinity Church off Goodramgate has delightful box pews and uneven floors. On the way back to Marygate, notice the round St Mary's Tower at its junction with Bootham. Part of the walls of St Mary's Abbey, it was blown up in 1644 during the Civil War and later rebuilt, rather inaccurately.

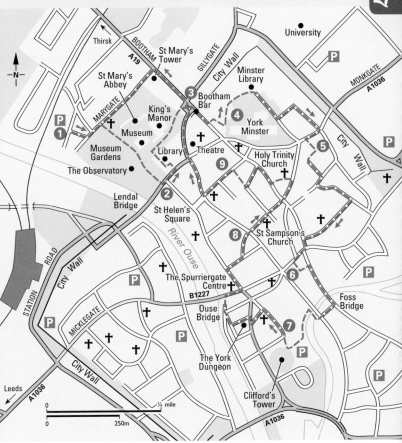

WALK 17 DIRECTIONS

❶ Walk back into Marygate, turn left, cross the road and enter Museum Gardens through the archway. Follow the path straight ahead, passing the Observatory, and leave the gardens by the lodge.

❷ Turn left, then left again towards the library. Go left through a gate, and along the side of the library. Go up the steps, and through a gate in the wall. At the bottom of the slope, turn right and follow Abbey Wall into Exhibition Square.

❸ Cross at the traffic-lights and go through Bootham Bar. A few paces on your left, take a passageway beside The Hole in the Wall pub and turn right down Precentor's Court. By the Minster, go left through the gate, signed 'York Minster Dean's Park'.

④ Follow the path left to the Minster Library building. Bend right through the gate and along the cobbled road. Turn left by the postbox down Chapter House Street, bending right into Ogleforth. At the crossroads turn right, then go left through an archway opposite The National Trust Café.

WHAT TO LOOK OUT FOR

Allow time to visit magnificent York Minster. The Undercroft is worth the admission fee to walk through the building's history, including Roman walls, some with painted plaster intact, and medieval foundations. Also visit The Treasury and the shrine of St William of York.

WHERE TO EAT AND DRINK

York is well supplied with places to eat, from fast-food snacks to gourmet meals. There are many good, characterful pubs, too. For wonderful surroundings, you can eat in the 18th-century Assembly Rooms in Blake Street.

⑤ Bear right into Bartle Garth, which bends left. At the T-junction turn right, and then go left down Spen Lane. Opposite Hilary House, go right along St Saviourgate. At the T-junction turn left, then right at the crossroads. Next to Jones's shoe shop on the left, take a passage, Lady Peckitt's Yard.

⑥ Go under the buildings, then turn left to Fossgate. Turn right, go over the bridge and then turn right along Merchantgate. At the T-junction, cross the road and take the glazed walkway beside the bridge, signed 'Castle Area', into the car park by Clifford's Tower.

⑦ Bend right and go to the right of the Hilton Hotel. Just after the church on the right, go left down Friargate, right along Clifford Street, and left by The York Dungeon. At the riverside turn right, ascend the steps by Ouse Bridge and turn right. At the traffic-lights, turn left by The Spurriergate Centre. By the NatWest Bank go right, forking left into Feasegate.

⑧ Go ahead to cross Parliament Street and pass St Sampson's Church. Go straight on at the next crossroads into Goodramgate. After 50yds (46m), go left through a gateway into Holy Trinity churchyard, and leave by a passage to the left of the tower, to reach Low Petergate. Turn right, then take the next left into Grape Lane. Where it bends left, turn right down the narrow Coffee Yard into Stonegate.

⑨ Go left to St Helen's Square and turn right by Lloyds TSB. Go straight on at the next crossroads back to Exhibition Square. At the traffic-lights, turn left up Bootham. Turn left down Marygate by the circular tower to return to the car park.

WHILE YOU'RE THERE

The Victorian Gothic architect Pugin called Yorkshire Museum in Museum Gardens a 'detestable building'; 'it would have been hardly possible,' he wrote, 'to have erected more offensive objects than these buildings in the immediate vicinity of one of the purest specimens of Christian architecture in the country.' Displays include Roman objects, sculpture from St Mary's Abbey, Viking remains and the medieval Middleham Jewel of finely-engraved gold.

Roseberry Topping and Captain Cook Country

An ascent of Roseberry Topping for fine views
and reminders of one of Britain's great explorers.

DISTANCE 5.5 miles (8.8km)	**MINIMUM TIME** 2hrs 30min

ASCENT/GRADIENT 1,214ft (370m) ▲▲▲ **LEVEL OF DIFFICULTY** +++

PATHS Hillside climb, then tracks and field paths, 5 stiles

LANDSCAPE One of the best 360-degree views in Yorkshire

SUGGESTED MAP OS Explorer OL 26 North York Moors – Western

START/FINISH Grid reference: NZ 570128

DOG FRIENDLINESS Off lead, except in farmland

PARKING Car park on A173 just south of Newton under Roseberry

PUBLIC TOILETS In car park at foot of Roseberry Topping

Visible for miles around and one of the most distinctive of all English hills, Roseberry Topping, 1,051ft (320m) high, was once an integral part of the North York Moors plateau. Over the millennia, however, the forces of nature eroded the land around it, but the Topping itself was protected by a cap of harder sandstone. In time it became an isolated conical hill, stranded above the plain of the River Tees. Through the centuries it has been called many things, from Odinburgh (after the Norse God) to Rosemary Torp (by the notoriously-inaccurate Daniel Defoe). Roseberry means 'fortress in the heath' and Topping, a 'point' – though there is no sign of a fortress there now.

Iron at Fault

Roseberry Topping retained its conical perfection until the night of 8th August 1912, when a huge chunk of land fell from its south-west slope and gave it the now-characteristic jagged profile. The immediate cause of the fall was the ironstone mining operations that had been burrowing into the slopes of the hill, since 1880, when the Roseberry Ironstone Company opened its first seam. Like much of this part of the North York Moors, Roseberry Topping is rich in ironstone, and it seemed a prize worth winning. The company survived for only three years, but the seam was later re-opened first by the Tees Furnace Company and then by its successor Burton and Sons. Burton's were blamed for the 1912 collapse, and for another landslide ten years later, but the topping is geologically unstable and could have slipped at any time.

Cook's Tours

After the descent from Roseberry Topping, and the climb again to the woodland, the track descends over Great Ayton Moor. Ahead, the Captain Cook Monument, a stone obelisk 51ft (15.5m) high, dominates the view. The great explorer was born in 1728 within sight of Roseberry Topping at Marton (then a village, but now a suburb of Middlesbrough) and went to school at nearby Great Ayton. The monument was erected in 1827, with

an inscription that names James Cook as 'amongst the most celebrated and most admired benefactors of the human race.' From 1736 his father worked at Aireyholme Farm (not open to the public), near Point **6** on the walk.

Mine Houses

Just after you have gone through the gate after Point **5**, the dips and hollows in the ground to the left are the remains of another ironstone mine, Ayton Banks. This was last worked in the 1920s. A little further on, you will pass Gribdale Terrace, a typical row of cottages built to house the iron miners and their families.

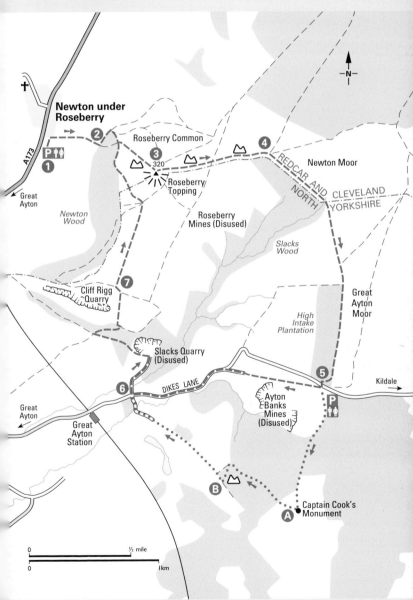

WALK 18 DIRECTIONS

1 Take the rough lane beside the car park towards Roseberry Topping. The path goes through a gateway then rises to a second gate at the beginning of the woodland.

2 Go through the gate into National Trust Land and turn left. There is a well-worn, mostly-paved, path to the summit. It is a stiff climb to the trig point on the top of the hill.

WHILE YOU'RE THERE

Roseberry Topping attracts more than 100,000 visitors each year, many of whom make it to the summit. As a result, it is in constant danger from erosion, both from those thousands of feet and from the sometimes severe weather that can affect the northern slope of the Moors. The National Trust, which owns it, needs to maintain a balance between access and conservation. You may find, therefore, that some parts are cordoned off, and access is limited to other areas. Stone and soil – in the last campaign more than 200 tonnes – are imported to try to stabilise the paths. Do your bit by making sure you stay on the tracks and obey any warning signs.

3 From the summit, walk east from the trig point, past two iron poles set into rock, and straight on along the paved way. Go steeply downhill. At the bottom, bear right to go up a track that bends right around the corner of woodland to a gate.

4 Go through the gate and take the path alongside the wood, following yellow waymarkers. Continue on the path until it eventually follows a wall and descends the hillside to reach a road.

WHERE TO EAT AND DRINK

There is often a refreshment caravan in the car park at the foot of Roseberry Topping, and an ice cream van up the lane. Otherwise, head for nearby Newton under Roseberry, where the King's Arms is recommended by locals for its atmosphere, and its meals – especially the puddings.

5 Turn right, cross the cattle grid and bear left between two benches, then go right, along the fence line, at first parallel with the road. Go down the field, through a gate and then over a stile and out into a lane. Walk past the cottages to reach a road, where you go straight ahead.

6 At a crossroads go right, down Aireyholme Lane. Follow the lane as it winds past houses, then take a signed footpath left over a stile. Follow the fence to two gates into woodland. After 0.5 mile (800m), go right at a National Trust sign, up a path ascending through the woods to a signposted stile. Over it, turn left to another stile, then after it, go right along the edge of the woodland. Bend left to a gate near a house.

7 Walk across two fields to a stile, then continue uphill to the tower. Beyond it, take a grassy path left down a gully, to a gate into woodland. Follow the path downhill through the woods to return to the gate at the top of the lane leading back to the car park.

Roseberry Topping – A Longer Walk

To get another perspective on Roseberry Topping, and to see the Monument to Captain Cook, take this extra loop.
See map and information panel for Walk 18

DISTANCE 7 miles (11.3km)	MINIMUM TIME 3hrs 15min
ASCENT/GRADIENT 1,640ft (500m) ▲▲▲	LEVEL OF DIFFICULTY ✦✦✧

WALK 19 DIRECTIONS
(Walk 18 option)

From Point **5** on the main walk, turn right, then left through a gate and up the track into Gribdale Forest. Follow the path for 0.5 mile (800m) to reach the Captain Cook Monument, Point **A**. There was national sorrow when Cook was killed in Hawaii in 1779, but it took another 49 years for this monument to be erected. He is described in the inscription as 'a man of nautical knowledge inferior to none, in zeal, prudence and energy superior to most.' It tells us he will be remembered 'while the art of navigation shall be cultivated… the spirit of enterprise, commerce and philanthropy shall animate the sons of Britain, [and] while it shall be deemed a Christian Nation to spread civilisation and the blessings of the Christian faith among pagan and savage tribes.'

The monument has lasted longer than the *North Eastern Daily Gazette*, whose readers subscribed in 1895 for its restoration. With superb views all around, it is a fitting monument to Cook – especially as his birthplace in Marton has long been demolished and his family's Great Ayton home was moved to Australia in 1934.

With your back to the inscription on the monument, walk half right along a path that passes through two standing stones. Go left, following the waymark where the path divides, and left again just beyond where the path forks. The path goes steeply down, eventually through woodland to reach a green track, Point **B**. Turn right then, after 200yds (183m), go left at a crossing. Walk down to a gate and continue downhill with a wall to your right, bending right on a track down towards a lake. Continue over a stile and along the footpath, then through a gate and along the track and on to a metalled lane, to reach a crossroads at Point **6** on the main walk, where you continue ahead.

> **WHAT TO LOOK OUT FOR**
> Visit Great Ayton, where you can see the schoolroom where Captain Cook studied between 1736 and 1741, and a rather mawkish statue of him as a boy on the attractive village green. Great Ayton has always been a strongly Quaker village, though the independent school they founded in 1824 has closed.

Vikings and a Cardinal Beside the Ouse

From Wistow to Cawood, and a return along the river bank, with reminders of 1066 and Cardinal Wolsey.

DISTANCE 7 miles (11.3km)	MINIMUM TIME 3hrs
ASCENT/GRADIENT Negligible ▲▲▲	LEVEL OF DIFFICULTY ✦✦✦

PATHS Field paths and tracks, river embankment, 4 stiles

LANDSCAPE Flat farmland and river flood plain

SUGGESTED MAP OS Explorer 290 York, Selby & Tadcaster

START/FINISH Grid reference: SE 596362

DOG FRIENDLINESS Dogs should be on lead at all times

PARKING Wide roadside by former railway bridge north-east of Wistow village

PUBLIC TOILETS None en route

WALK 20 DIRECTIONS

From the parking place by the former railway bridge, walk towards the village, turning right at the T-junction. Bear left past the school and right between two 'no entry' signs to pass the church and The Black Swan public house. At the road junction beyond, turn left along Station Road. At the next junction, turn right. Where the road bends left, go straight ahead up a track by a footpath sign. Where the track divides, go right and follow the hedgerow round to the right, following a yellow waymarker.

The path goes half left across the field to the end of a hedge and crosses a ditch. Go straight ahead with another ditch on your right. A little way down, go left over a footbridge and turn left along the field-edge. After 50yds (46m), go left over another footbridge with a stile at the end. Go straight ahead with, first, a ditch on your right. In the second field, bear slightly left to a metal gate in a hedge. Beyond, the path goes

straight towards the red-brick house and then on to a lane. This is fertile farming country, on the rich flood plain of the River Ouse. A wide variety of crops is grown, including sugar beet, which you may see later being transported by barge along the river.

Turn right, then go left beyond the house, up the field side to cross a footbridge. Turn right and walk down the field-edge. The path becomes a grassy track and emerges on to a road. Turn right. Just beyond Park View Farm and Livery, go over a stile on the right and bear left to follow a track that goes to the left of a paddock. By playing fields, go through a hedge

WHERE TO EAT AND DRINK

The Black Swan in Wistow has bar meals and a restaurant (and also runs the village post office, serving light refreshments). Wistow also has a fish and chip shop. In Cawood, the Ferry Inn, which has been voted Pub of the Year several times by the local newspaper, offers home-cooked food and real ale.

WISTOW

gap and turn right to a footpath sign. Follow the fenced path to a road. Turn left and left again at a junction. Go straight on to the road head, turning right beyond the last house to follow a path to the main street. Turn left. At a T-junction, turn right, signed 'York'. Follow the road past the gatehouse to Cawood Castle.

This is all that remains of the former seat of the Archbishops of York, on a site given to them by King Athelstan around AD 930. The gatehouse is 15th century, and is now let for holidays by the Landmark Trust. Cawood was home to Cardinal Wolsey, and it was here that he was arrested for treason against King Henry VIII. It was the nearest Wolsey ever got to York, even though he was its archbishop.

At the traffic-lights, turn right and, just before the bridge, go right again, down Old Road. Where the road bends right, continue ahead down Water Row to a gate. Do not enter the churchyard but turn left, then right before the gate to pass to the left of the church. Walk along the river bank for 3.25 miles (5.3km). As the river bends southwards you are opposite Riccall Landing. This is where the Norwegian fleet of Harald Hardrada landed in 1066, in its attempt to defeat King Harold Godwinson. Three hundred fearsome Viking ships were sailed or rowed up the Ouse, and after the troops disembarked, they marched to Stamford Bridge where, though superior in numbers, they were defeated by the English army. Of the 300 ships, only two dozen sailed back to Norway. Beyond a brick building with a footbridge to it, turn right at a crossing track, passing a pond. Turn left at the T-junction and follow the road back to the start.

Monks and an Astronomer at Byland Abbey

From the romantic ruins of Byland Abbey to an old observatory – and back through the fish pond.

DISTANCE *5 miles (8km)*   MINIMUM TIME *2hrs 30min*

ASCENT/GRADIENT *623ft (190m)* ▲▲▲   LEVEL OF DIFFICULTY ✦✦✦

PATHS *Woodland tracks, field paths, 8 stiles*

LANDSCAPE *Undulating pasture and woodland on slopes of Hambleton Hills*

SUGGESTED MAP *OS Explorer OL 26 North York Moors – Western*

START/FINISH *Grid reference: SE 548789*

DOG FRIENDLINESS *Dogs can be off lead in woodland where indicated*

PARKING *Car park beside Abbey Inn in Byland for abbey visitors*

PUBLIC TOILETS *At Byland Abbey*

In 1134 a party of Savigniac monks set out from their English mother house in Furness on the west coast of Cumbria to found a new monastery. Forty-three years and six moves later, Byland was founded as their permanent home, and by then they had become part of the Cistercian Order. The final move was from nearby Stocking, where they had settled in 1147. The relocation to Byland in 1177 must have been long planned, for Byland's earliest buildings, the lay brothers' quarters, were complete by 1165; everything had to be in order for the arrival of the monks themselves.

The Abbey Buildings

The most impressive parts of the ruins remaining today are in the church – and especially the remnants of the fine rose window in the west front. Beneath it, the main door leads into the nave, the lay brothers' portion of the church. The monks used the east end. Although the walls of the south transept collapsed in 1822, that area of the church still retains one of Byland's greatest treasures – the geometrically tiled floors, with their delicate patterns in red, cream and black.

Work and Pray

The monks at Byland Abbey, like all of their Cistercian brethren, rose at about 2am for the first service, Vigil. Two more services and a meeting followed before they had lunch at midday. They spent the afternoon working at their allotted tasks, and there were three more services, after which they went to bed, at around 8:30pm. The choir monks did some of the manual work in the abbey and on its estate, but the Cistercians also had lay brothers to work for them.

The lay brothers were vital to the success of the monasteries. They also took vows (though much simpler ones than the monks) and had their own church services. The Black Death in the 14th century, which radically changed the supply of agricultural labour, effectively ended the tradition of lay brothers in English monasteries.

Oldstead Observatory

At the highest point of the walk is Oldstead Observatory, built on the splendidly-named Mount Snever by John Wormald, who lived at Oldstead Hall in the valley below. It was a celebration, as the rather worn inscription tells us, of Queen Victoria's accession to the throne. At just over 40ft (12m) high, 1,146ft (349m) above sea level, it is high enough to scan the heavens, though history does not record if Mr Wormald made any startling astronomical discoveries through his roof-mounted telescope.

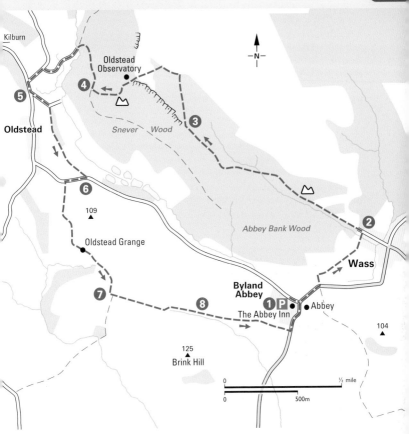

WALK 21 DIRECTIONS

❶ Visit the abbey, then leave beside the ticket office and turn right along the abbey's north side. Opposite a public footpath sign, go left through a gateway and after 10yds (9m) right, over a stile. Cross the field to a second stile, then bear half left uphill to a waymarked gate behind a bench. Go through two more gates and on to a metalled lane.

❷ Turn left. At the top of the lane go through a gate signed 'Cam Farm, Observatory'. The path climbs then leaves the wood edge to rise to a terrace. After a stile, take the left-hand path, following Cam Farm. Go straight on at two junctions, uphill, to reach a large open space.

❸ Turn right and, just before a waymarked metal gate, turn left along the wood edge. Follow the path to Oldstead Observatory, bearing left through the wood. Pass to the left of the Observatory, go down a slope and follow the path running steeply downhill to reach a signpost.

❹ Turn right on the track, signed 'Oldstead'. Follow the track as it curves left to become a metalled lane. Turn left at the T-junction, and left again on to the road by a seat. Just before the road narrows sign, turn left.

❺ Go through some gateposts and over a cattle grid. Then, as the avenue of trees ends, take a signposted footpath to the right, uphill. Climb up to a stile, bending around to the left beside the woodland to a gate. After the next gate, go straight ahead, through two more gates and on to a metalled road.

WHAT TO LOOK OUT FOR

The lumps and bumps of the final field you cross on the walk are the remains of the monks' ponds. It is difficult to visualise the abbey in the Middle Ages almost surrounded by water. There was a large pond that stretched almost 0.5 mile (800m) from east to west, to the north of the abbey buildings, which was used to flush the drains, and two more south and south-east. To the south-west, where this walk passes through, was a roughly triangular pond, bounded by a bank supporting the abbey's mill. The ponds were also used for breeding fish, one of the most important staples of the monks' diet. They practised large-scale fish farming at nearby Oldstead Grange.

❻ Turn right then, just beyond the road sign which indicates a bend, take a track to the left by the Oldstead Grange sign. Pass the house and go between barns

WHERE TO EAT AND DRINK

There are two country inns with good food on the walk. The Abbey Inn in Byland, directly opposite the abbey, has old beams and flagged floors, and offers sandwiches and meals at lunchtime, and fine dinners. The Wombwell Arms at Wass is also noted for its good food. Both places serve good traditional Yorkshire beers.

and through a gateway. Bear right downhill on the track, bending right on a track to a gateway with a waymarked tree.

❼ Immediately after the gateway, turn left and go through the wood to a Byland Abbey signpost. Follow the path ahead as it bends left by another sign, go over a stile and down the field with the hedge on your left, bending left then right at the end to another signpost. Go through an opening beside a metal gate and along the field with a hedge on your right.

WHILE YOU'RE THERE

Take a trip to nearby Kilburn to visit the Mouseman Visitor Centre. Here Robert Thompson, born in 1876, worked at his now-famous furniture, each piece carved with his characteristic mouse. Oak furniture is still made by his successors, and the centre demonstrates the history of the firm and its work.

❽ Go over two stiles then bear slightly left to another stile. Go across the field to a signpost in the hedge by a metal gate. Follow the fence, then go on to the road by a wooden stile. Turn left back to the car park opposite the abbey.

A Whirl Around Whorlton and Swainby

From the once-industrial village of Swainby, a walk with fine views from the Moors and a taste of history in Whorlton.

DISTANCE	6 miles (9.7km) MINIMUM TIME 3hrs
ASCENT/GRADIENT	1,098ft (335m) ▲▲▲ LEVEL OF DIFFICULTY ✦✦✦
PATHS	Tracks and moorland paths, lots of bracken, 6 stiles
LANDSCAPE	Farmland and moorland, with some woodland
SUGGESTED MAP	OS Explorer OL 26 North York Moors – Western
START/FINISH	Grid reference: NZ 477020
DOG FRIENDLINESS	On short lead on moorland
PARKING	Roadside parking in Swainby village
PUBLIC TOILETS	In Swainby village

The charming and peaceful village street of Swainby, divided by its tree-lined stream, gives few hints of its dramatic past. It owes its existence to tragedy, the coming of plague – the Black Death – in the 14th century, when the inhabitants of the original village, just up the hill at Whorlton, deserted their homes and moved here. There may already have been a few houses here as Swainby means the village of the land workers, and is recorded in the 13th century. In the 19th century, Swainby was shocked out of its peaceful, rural existence by the opening of the ironstone mines in Scugdale. The village took on many of the aspects of an American frontier town, becoming full of miners and their equipment, and awash with their smoke and clatter.

Jet Propelled

As well as ironstone, jet was mined in the Swainby area in the 19th century, including on Whorl Hill, which you will walk around. Most of the jet pits were small, employing no more than a dozen men, but they could be very profitable, especially during the boom time for jet, encouraged by the example of Queen Victoria's black mourning jewellery. Like coal, jet is fossilised wood. It comes in two types, hard and soft; hard jet was probably formed in sea water and soft jet in fresh water. It has been prized for more than 3,000 years, and was known to the Celts as Freya's Tears. Because it is easy to work and takes a fine polish, jet workshops could turn out large quantities of jewellery relatively quickly. Although some jet objects are still made, especially in Whitby, the industry had virtually died out by the 1920s.

Church and Castle

The path from Whorl Hill takes us into the deserted village of Whorlton. Little survived its abandonment after the Black Death except the church and the castle, both now partially ruined. On any but a sunny day, Holy Cross Church can be a disturbing place, with its avenue of yew trees leading to the arches of the nave, now open to the skies. The chancel is roofed, and a flap in the doorway allows you to look inside to see a fine early 14th-century oak figure of a knight. It is probably Nicholas, Lord Maynell, who fought with Edward I in Wales and hunted in the woods here. The gatehouse of Maynell's castle, just along the road, is the only substantial part left. It was built at the end of the 14th century, and was besieged 250 years later during the Civil War. You can still see on the walls the marks of cannon balls from the Parliamentarians' guns. East of the castle, which occupied more than 6 acres (2.4 ha), are further earthworks, which protected the fortified village.

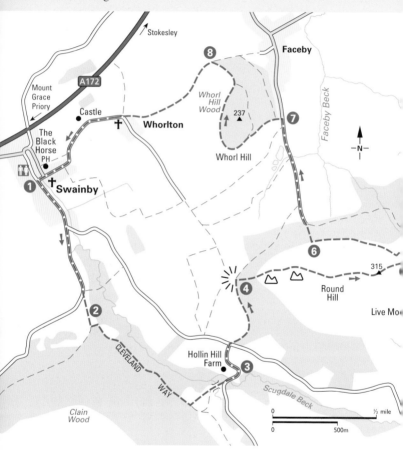

WALK 22 DIRECTIONS

❶ With the church on your left, walk down the village street to the right of the stream. Continue walking past a sign 'Unsuitable for Buses and Coaches' and go straight ahead uphill. As the road bends to the right, follow the bridleway sign to Scugdale, up the track that lies ahead.

❷ Go through a gate and turn left to join the waymarks for the Cleveland Way National Trail. Walk through the woodland, turning left, just after a seat, down to a gate. The footpath goes half right, towards blue-topped posts and downhill to another gate. Cross the stream on the footbridge to reach a lane, with another footbridge, over Scugdale Beck. Turn left.

SWAINBY

❸ Follow the lane past Hollin Hill Farm to a T-junction with telephone and post boxes. Cross the lane and go through a Cleveland Way signed gate. Walk up the path beside woodland to a gate (there's a view of the valley from this ridge).

❹ The path beyond bends right to a stile and goes on to a paved track in the wood. Go straight ahead at a crossing track to another gate, and continue to follow the paved path up to the heather moorland, passing a cairn. After the first summit, the path descends beyond a large and a small cairn into a dip. Just before the paved path ends, look out for a narrow path off to the left, down through the heather.

WHERE TO EAT AND DRINK
Blackmith's in Swainby, a pub established in 1775, offers good beer and an extensive menu – though it no longer offers to shoe your horse. The Black Horse in the High Street is also noted for its beer.

❺ After about 100yds (91m) you will reach a concrete post. Bear left and follow the narrow path down the gully to a fence beside a wood. Turn left to a signpost. Go straight on, eventually going over a spoil heap to reach a gate on your right.

❻ Through the gate, go straight down the hill through woodland. At

WHILE YOU'RE THERE
Spend a moment of solitude at nearby Mount Grace Priory, the best preserved of England's charterhouses – communities of Carthusian monks. There's a reconstructed monk's cell showing how they lived as hermits, coming together rarely except for services in the church. Their isolation was such that even their meals were served through an L-shaped hatch so they couldn't see who brought them.

the bottom, bear right, then left to cross a stile by a gate and go down the lane. Just after the first house on the left, take a footpath over two stiles.

❼ Walk up through the woodland on to a grassy track. Turn left, and left again at another track. At a T-junction, turn left again and follow the track downhill to a stile. Turn left to go over another stile. Go straight ahead along the signed track.

❽ Go over a stile beside a gate and follow the track along the hillside. Over a stile with steps beyond, turn left at the bottom and follow the field-edge. Go through a gateway beside a paddock to another gateway on to a metalled lane. Follow the lane past Whorlton church and castle back to Swainby village.

WHAT TO LOOK OUT FOR
From the highest part of the walk, which takes you up on to the northern edge of the North York Moors plateau, you are rewarded with extensive northward views over the vast industrial complexes surrounding Middlesbrough. It was the production of iron from the hills which really put Middlesbrough on the map; it had a population of just 40 in 1829, 7,600 in 1851, when the first blast furnace opened, and 20,000 nine years later. Prime Minister Gladstone called the town 'an infant Hercules'. Beyond the River Tees, the area of Seal Sands is home to an oil refinery and chemical works. It's the terminal of the 220-mile (354 km) pipeline bringing oil and gas from the Ekofisk field in the North Sea. If you are on the hills at dawn or dusk, you may see the flare stacks glowing on the skyline.

Out on the Tiles at Boltby and Thirlby Bank

*Looking out for village mosaics and distant views
on a quiet section of the Cleveland Way National Trail.*

DISTANCE *5.25 miles (8.4km)*   MINIMUM TIME *2hrs*

ASCENT/GRADIENT *656ft (200m)* ▲▲▲   LEVEL OF DIFFICULTY +++

PATHS *Mostly easy field and woodland paths; very steep and muddy climb up Thirlby Bank, 4 stiles*

LANDSCAPE *Farmland, woodland and moorland ridge*

SUGGESTED MAP *OS Explorer OL 26 North York – Western*

START/FINISH *Grid reference: SE 490866*

DOG FRIENDLINESS *Dogs should be on lead throughout but can probably be off on Cleveland Way*

PARKING *Roadside parking in Boltby village*

PUBLIC TOILETS *None en route*

The western boundary of the North York Moors National Park passes just outside the village of Boltby. It is a delightful, small-scale place, with a tiny 19th-century chapel and stone-built houses with red, pantiled roofs typical of the area. Despite its size, it used to have two pubs, as well as a tailor, a shoemaker, a butcher, a blacksmith and three masons. The single village street is crossed by the Gurtof Beck – pedestrians have their own ancient humpbacked stone bridge, from where the walk begins.

Mosaic Trail

As you begin the walk you will notice a glittering mosaic of a kingfisher on a wall beside the Gurtof Beck. This is one of 23 that mark points on the Hambleton Hillside Mosaic Walk. This 36-mile (58km) route begins at the National Park visitor centre at Sutton Bank, and winds its way on and off the ridge. Further on in the walk you'll come across a tiled picture of a red-capped mushroom on a tree stump, and a search of Boltby village on your return will yield a dragonfly and a worm-eating mole.

Moat and Park

The farm at Tang Hall has more ancient origins than you might think. Just before you reach it, you will notice deep ditches beside the path, sometimes filled with water. These are the remains of a moat which once surrounded a medieval manor house on the site. A little further on, the parkland of Southwoods Hall is typical of the managed landscapes of the 18th century. There are fine beech, lime and larch trees, as well as a cedar of Lebanon.

Beyond Southwoods Hall, the walk passes through Midge Holme Gate and into woodland. This is very much pheasant country, and you are likely to flush out one or two of these noisy birds during the walk. Most characteristic is the male common pheasant, with its iridescent neck feathers of blue and green, its red wattles and long, arching tail. In contrast to the cock, the hen is duller – mottled brown and with a shorter tail.

They are heavily protected from predators and poachers in these woods by gamekeepers, and kept well-fed during the winter months so that plenty survive for the shooting season, which begins on 1st October each year.

Fort and Lost

On top of Boltby Scar, just as you begin to descend from the Cleveland Way back to the village, are the scant remains of a Bronze Age hill-fort, one of several along the edge of the Moors. It was 2.5 acres (1ha) in extent, and surrounded by an earth rampart and ditch on three of its five sides – the others were protected by the cliffs. It was mostly destroyed by ploughing in the late 1950s.

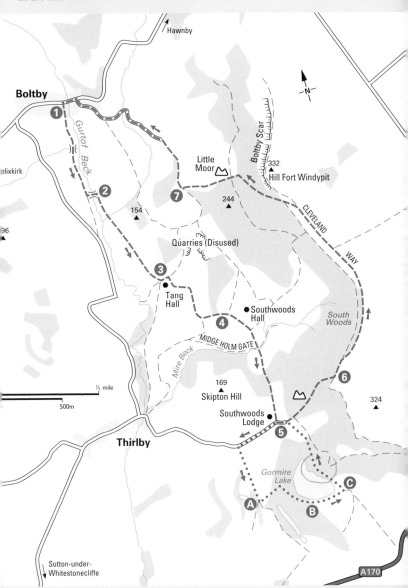

WALK 23

WALK 23 DIRECTIONS

1 From the humpback bridge in the centre of Boltby village, follow the signed public footpath along the stream to a gate, and through three more gates to pass over a small footbridge to a stile. Continue following the stream; cross a gated footbridge, go over a stile and through a gate, then bear left over the stream and right to a gated stone footbridge.

2 Cross the bridge and continue over two stiles, then go straight on, beside the hedge, to go through two gates on to a metalled track at Tang Hall.

3 Turn left and, at the end of the farm buildings, turn right by a sign to Southwoods and through a gate to go diagonally left across the field; the route is marked by stones. At the end of the field, go through two gates then continue with a wire fence on your right. The path veers left and descends to a gate.

4 Continue along the track to a handgate. Go straight ahead on a track, confusingly named Midge Holm Gate. Follow the track to reach another gate beside a cottage, Southwoods Lodge, and go on to a metalled lane.

5 Turn left, following the track, signed 'Bridleway to Gormire'. At the signpost go straight ahead

on the bridleway, up Thirlby Bank. This steep and often muddy track ascends the ridge; bear right at the fork part way up. Eventually you will reach a Cleveland Way sign on the ridge top.

6 Turn left and follow the Cleveland Way footpath for about a mile (1.6km) along the ridge, until you reach a bridleway sign to Boltby to the left. Descend to a gate then go straight ahead on the woodland ride, crossing a track to a gate. Continue ahead down the field, through a gate, and follow the track round to the right, along the edge of a wood.

7 At a signpost, turn right towards Boltby, to continue to a gate. Pass a tree stump with a mosaic of a toadstool and descend to a gate on to a lane. Follow the lane through another gate. Cross the stream by a footbridge and continue up the metalled lane. At the T-junction in the village, turn left back to the humpback bridge where the walk began.

Boltby and the Remote Gormire Lake

An extended version of Walk 23 visits Gormire Lake, an unusual survivor from the ice ages.

See map and information panel for Walk 23

DISTANCE *1.25 miles (2km)*   MINIMUM TIME *3hrs 30min*
ASCENT/GRADIENT *754ft (230m)* ▲▲▲   LEVEL OF DIFFICULTY **+++**

WALK 24 DIRECTIONS
(Walk 23 option)

Gormire Lake is one of very few truly natural stretches of open water in North Yorkshire.

At Point **5** in Walk 23, at Southwoods Lodge, turn right on the metalled lane. After 0.25 mile (400m), turn left through a gate before houses, and down a track. Go through a metal handgate beside a farm gate and follow the fence through another handgate. Follow the fence as it bears left by a waymark (Point **A**), and continue with the hedge on the left. The path descends through woodland, over a wooden stile, bearing left after it.

Continue through woodland, now climbing, following a sign to Gormire, eventually descending to the water's edge, Point **B**.

Gormire was formed after the last ice age, when meltwater from the ice sheet that covered the Vale of York found its way blocked and collected in the depression formed. Accessible only on foot, the lake is edged in summer with a wide variety of plants including the tufted loosestrife. Among the birds that you may see is the great crested grebe. In the dusk, beware if you hear the sound of horses;

Gormire is said to be haunted by the ghost of a knight who tricked the Abbot of Rievaulx into lending him a horse, and plunged over Whitestone Cliff to his death in the lake, pursued by the devil.

At the water's edge you should turn right to reach a signpost, Point **C**. Follow the footpath sign left to continue along the other side of the lake, to another signpost near Point **5** on the main walk. Turn right to ascend Thirlby Bank.

Overleaf: View of the countryside around Lake Gormire (Walk 24)

The Brontës at Thorpe Underwood

In the footsteps of Anne and Branwell Brontë, who spent time near Thorpe.

DISTANCE *4 miles (6.4km)*   MINIMUM TIME *2hrs*

ASCENT/GRADIENT *Negligible* ▲▲▲   LEVEL OF DIFFICULTY ✦✦✦

PATHS *Field paths and lanes, 5 stiles*

LANDSCAPE *Flat farmland*

SUGGESTED MAP *OS Explorer 289 Leeds, Harrogate, Wetherby & Pontefract*

START/FINISH *Grid reference: SE 458591*

DOG FRIENDLINESS *Dogs should be on lead except on metalled tracks around Green Hammerton*

PARKING *Open parking area just before Fishermans Lodge Café*

PUBLIC TOILETS *None en route*

WALK 25 DIRECTIONS

Walk along the lane with the Fisherman Lodge Café to your left, to reach a Green Hammerton footpath sign on the right by a high brick wall. This is the edge of the Thorpe Underwood Estate. Now home to an independent school, Queen Ethelburga's College, Thorpe Underwood Hall was rebuilt in 1912 on the site of the former Thorp Green Hall, where Anne Brontë was governess to the four children of the Revd Edmund Robinson from 1840 to 1845. The original house appears as Horton Lodge in her novel *Agnes Grey*. Anne had mixed feelings about her position. While she liked the

WHERE TO EAT AND DRINK

There is nowhere directly on the route, though The Bay Horse in Green Hammerton is nearby. It serves real ale and has a beer garden. Food is served at lunchtime and in the evening. The Angler Inn at Lower Dunsforth has a good local reputation for its home-cooked food.

children, she hated being away from her home in Haworth – her poem Lines Written at Thorp Green tells of her loneliness here.

Go over the stile beside the wall and follow the path between the hedge and wall to a stile and footbridge. In 1843, Anne's brother Branwell came to Thorp Green. He was engaged as tutor to the Robinson's boy. Branwell was ill while he was there – but not so unwell that he was unable to instigate some sort of illicit relationship with Mrs Robinson, 13 years his senior. Her husband found out and Branwell was dismissed in July 1845; Anne had resigned a month earlier. Branwell's dismissal led to his alcoholism and drug use, which led to his early death three years later.

Go over the footbridge and follow the waymarked path diagonally left across the field to pass between two oak trees and through a gap in a fence. Follow the path with the hedge on your left, bending right at the end. After 200yds (183m),

THORPE UNDERWOOD

down a metalled lane. Where the lane bends left, go straight ahead through a gateway towards Pool Spring Farm and continue along the track for 0.75 miles (1.2km). The track bends left, to pass right of the farm buildings. By the farm turn right and follow the track as it bends left, then right. Continue along the track. This is part of the route by which Anne Brontë would have made her way from Thorp Green Hall to the railway at Cattal, on the York to Harrogate line, for her rare visits back to her home at the parsonage in Haworth.

Where the main track swings left, go straight on up another track, through a gateway. The track passes beside woodland to a handgate by a metal gate and comes out on to a lane. Go straight ahead to reach a high brick wall. Behind the wall, and just visible a little further on, through Gate H, is the 'new' Hall, designed in 1912 by York architect Walter Brierley, 'the Lutyens of the North'. The site of Thorp Green Hall was just to the north-east of it, overlooking a large circular fishpond, of which Anne Brontë had a view from her room.

turn left over a waymarked footbridge in the hedge opposite. Go over the stile at the end of the bridge and follow the hedge on your right, over another two stiles and a footbridge.

Continue beside a small wood to a waymark post, then straight ahead across the field towards the farm buildings. The path curves to pass to the right of the buildings. After passing through a gateway, turn left

Follow the wall to a T-junction and turn left. Continue to follow the brick wall, turning left again at the next T-junction, just beyond the post box, and continue along the lane back to the parking place.

Herriot's Darrowby

*James Herriot based his fictional home town
on his real one — Thirsk.*

DISTANCE *5 miles (8km)*   MINIMUM TIME *2hrs*

ASCENT/GRADIENT *66ft (20m)* ▲▲▲   LEVEL OF DIFFICULTY +++

PATHS *Town paths, field paths and tracks, 6 stiles*

LANDSCAPE *Streamside and undulating pastureland around town*

SUGGESTED MAP *OS Explorer 302 Northallerton & Thirsk*

START/FINISH *Grid reference: SE 430813*

DOG FRIENDLINESS *Keep dogs on lead*

PARKING *Roadside parking in the main street of Sowerby village*

PUBLIC TOILETS *Thirsk town centre*

The elegant Georgian village street of Sowerby — now joined on to the town of Thirsk — is lined with a handsome avenue of lime trees. Such a civilised aspect belies the origins of the village's name, for Sowerby means the 'township in the muddy place'. Once you begin the walk, the reason becomes evident, even in dry weather. Sowerby is on the edge of the flood plain of the Cod Beck. Sowerby Flatts, which you will see across the beck at the start of the walk, and cross at the finish, is a popular venue for impromptu games of soccer and other sports, but is still prone to flooding.

Between Old and New

Once you've crossed the road by the end of New Bridge, you are walking between Old Thirsk and New Thirsk — though new in this context still means medieval. Old Thirsk is set to the east of the Cod Beck; like Sowerby, it too has a watery name, for Thirsk comes from an old Swedish word meaning a 'fen'. New Thirsk, to the west, is centred on the fine cobbled market place. The parish church, which you will pass twice, is the best Perpendicular church in North Yorkshire, with a particularly imposing tower.

South Kilvington, at the northern end of the walk, used to be a busy village on the main road north from Thirsk to Yarm. For much of the 19th century it was home to William Kingsley, who was vicar here until his death at the age of 101 in 1916 — having been born as Wellington defeated Napoleon at Waterloo. He entertained both the painter Turner and the art critic John Ruskin here — as well as his cousin Charles Kingsley, author of *The Water Babies*. More than a little eccentric, the vicar had signs in his garden saying 'Beware of Mantraps'. When asked where they were, he paraded his three housemaids.

Darrowby and Wight

For many visitors, the essential place to visit in Thirsk is Skeldale House in Kirkgate — on the right as you return from the church to the Market Square. This was the surgery of local vet James Wight — better known by his pen name, James Herriot. Now an award-winning museum, The World of James

THIRSK

Herriot, this was where Wight worked for all his professional life. Thirsk itself is a major character in the books, appearing lightly disguised as Darrowby. The museum has reconstructions of what the surgery and the family rooms were like in the 1940s, and tells the history of veterinary science. Whether or not you're a fan of the Herriot tales, which began with *If Only They Could Talk* in 1970, you'll find it a fascinating and nostalgic tour.

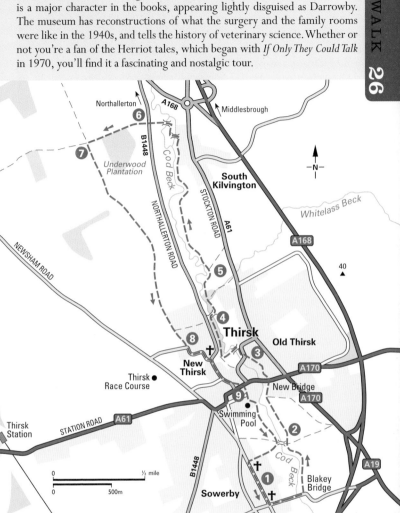

WALK 26 DIRECTIONS

❶ Walk down the village street, away from Thirsk. Just past the Methodist Church on the left, go left down Blakey Lane. Cross the bridge, turn left on a signed path and follow the stream, going through two kissing gates to a footbridge.

❷ Continue beside the stream to a stile. Go through two gates to a car park and ahead to the road.

Cross and take a path that curves left, then right by the bridge. At a paved area, turn right to go alongside a green to a road.

❸ Cross the road and continue ahead, crossing a main road and going left at the top of the green. Cross the metal bridge and continue beside the beck by the church. Before reaching the road take the path to the right, beside a bench, to a footbridge on the right.

WALK 26

④ Cross the bridge and go straight ahead through two gates, curving left to follow the beck to a gate by a bridge. Go straight ahead (not over the bridge) and follow the path across the fields, veering diagonally right to a stile on your right.

⑤ Go over the stile and follow the stream, going over another two stiles to pass beside houses. Continue left over a footbridge by some mill buildings. The path winds right to cross a second footbridge. Follow the bridleway sign across the field through a gate to reach the main road.

⑥ Cross the road and go through a signed gate opposite, to another gate beside a wood. 150yds (137m) after the wood, turn left at a waymark.

⑦ Walk down the field with a hedge on your left. In the second field, go left over a stile and continue with the hedge on your right, bearing half left to another stile. Continue across the field, then down the next field-edge, bearing left, then right at the end to a path that becomes a grassy lane between hedges.

⑧ At a road go straight ahead, bearing left, then right past the church. Turn right and walk into the town centre. In the Market Place, cross by the clock tower towards the Golden Fleece. Go down a signed passageway two premises to the pub's left, cross a lane and go down Villa Place.

⑨ Bear left to pass the swimming pool. Turn right and bend round the pool building to a gate. Go ahead to a gate and parallel with the beck. At the bridge, turn right across the field on a grassy track to a gate on to a lane, then straight ahead back to Sowerby.

A Medieval Walk from Fountains

*From the magnificent ruins of Fountains Abbey
to the fascinating medieval manor of Markenfield Hall.*

DISTANCE *6.5 miles (10.4km)*   MINIMUM TIME *3hrs*

ASCENT/GRADIENT *328ft (100m)* ▲▲▲   LEVEL OF DIFFICULTY ✦✦✦

PATHS *Field paths and tracks, a little road walking, 3 stiles*

LANDSCAPE *Farmland and woodland*

SUGGESTED MAP *OS Explorer 298 Nidderdale*

START/FINISH *Grid reference: SE 270681*

DOG FRIENDLINESS *Dogs should be on lead on field paths*

PARKING *Car park at west end of abbey, or at visitor centre*

PUBLIC TOILETS *Fountains Abbey visitor centre*

After you have climbed the hill from the car park and begun the walk along the valley side, following the ancient abbey wall, the south front of Fountains Hall is below you. Built by Sir Stephen Proctor in 1611, it is a fine Jacobean house, with lots of mullioned windows and cross gables. Were it anywhere other than at the entrance to Fountains Abbey, it would be seen as one of the great houses of the age. Sir Stephen was, by all accounts, not the most scrupulous of men, having made his huge fortune as Collector of Fines on Penal Statutes. Nor did he respect the Abbey buildings; the stone he built his house with was taken from the south-east corner of the monastic remains.

Abbey and Abbot

A little further along the path, the abbey ruins come into view. When monks from St Mary's Abbey in York first settled here in 1132, it was a wild and desolate place. Nevertheless their abbey prospered, and became one of the country's richest and most powerful Cistercian monasteries. More remains of Fountains than of any other abbey ruin in the country. Its church was 360ft (110m) long. The other buildings, laid out along (and over) the River Skell, give a vivid impression of what life was like here in the Middle Ages. All came to an end in 1539 when King Henry VIII dissolved the larger monasteries. This was only a few years after Abbot Marmaduke Huby had built the huge tower, a symbol of what he believed was the enduring power of his abbey.

Mr Aislabie's Garden

Beyond Fountains Abbey are the pleasure gardens laid out between 1716 and 1781 by John Aislabie and his son William. John had retired to his estate here at Studley Royal after being involved – as Chancellor of the Exchequer – in the financial scandal of the South Sea Bubble. It is one of the great gardens of Europe, contrasting green lawn with stretches of water, both formal and informal. Carefully placed in the landscape are ornamental buildings, from classical temples to Gothic towers. The Aislabie's mansion stood at the north end of the park; it was destroyed by fire in 1945.

FOUNTAINS ABBEY

The highlight of the southern end of the walk is Markenfield Hall, a rare early 14th-century fortified manor house, built around 1310 for the Markenfield family. You can see the tomb of Sir Thomas Markenfield and his wife Dionisia in Ripon Cathedral. Open for four weeks in the summer, the house still clearly demonstrates how a medieval knight and his family lived; it is part home, part farm. You can see the chapel and the great hall. The gatehouse, convincingly medieval, is 200 years younger than the house.

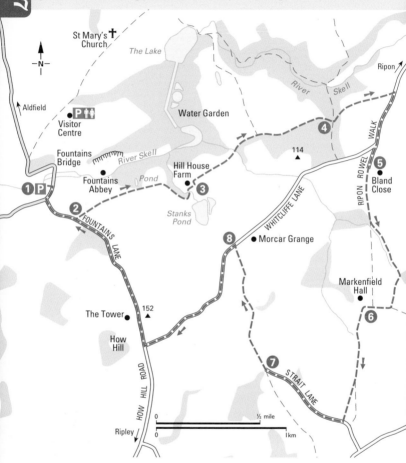

WALK 27 DIRECTIONS

❶ From the car park turn right uphill, signed 'Harrogate'. At the fork go left, signed 'Markington, Harrogate'. Just after the road bends right, go left at a footpath sign through a gate.

❷ Follow the grassy path just inside the ancient abbey wall, past a small pond. Go through a waymarked gate and follow the track as it curves round to the right through another gate, then bend left to a gate into Hill House Farm.

❸ Turn right then follow the footpath signs to go left at the end of a large shed and then right. Go through a metal gate on to a track. At the end of the hedge, go ahead down the field to a gate into the

FOUNTAINS ABBEY

wood. Follow the track, passing the ruined archway, to descend to a crossroads of tracks.

4 Go straight on, signed 'Ripon'. The track climbs to a gate with a Ripon Rowel Walk sign. Follow the track beside the line of trees to a gate on to Whitcliffe Lane. Turn right. At the top of the rise go straight ahead on the metalled road.

5 Go over the cattle grid by Bland Close, then leave the lane to go straight ahead with the hedge on your right to a gateway. Continue along the waymarked track, eventually with woodland to your right. Follow the park wall through a gateway to reach a gate on to a lane. Turn right to reach some farm buildings by Markenfield Hall.

6 Follow the wall to the left, going through a metal gate and straight ahead down the track, over a stile by a gate. Follow the track, then a waymark sign, across a field to a stile by a gate. Turn right up the narrow Strait Lane, to emerge into a field.

7 Follow the waymarked path beside the hedge. Go through a gate in the field corner and continue ahead with the hedge to the right. Go through two more gates. At a third gate, do not go through, but bend left through a hedge gap and down the field side, with the hedge on your right, to go through a gate on to Whitcliffe Lane.

8 Turn left and follow the lane, which leads in the direction of How Hill Tower, an 18th-century folly, to a T-junction. Turn right here and follow the road back to the car park.

Richmond's Drummer Boy

Following in the steps of the Richmond Drummer, to Easby Abbey.

DISTANCE 6 miles (9.7km) **MINIMUM TIME** 2hrs 20min

ASCENT/GRADIENT 656ft (200m) ▲▲▲ **LEVEL OF DIFFICULTY** ✦✦✦

PATHS Field and riverside paths, a little town walking, 15 stiles

LANDSCAPE Valley of River Swale and its steep banks

SUGGESTED MAP OS Explorer 304 Darlington & Richmond

START/FINISH Grid reference: NZ 168012

DOG FRIENDLINESS Dogs should be on lead for most of walk

PARKING Friars Close long-stay car park

PUBLIC TOILETS Friars Close car park, Richmond town centre and Round Howe car park

---

The first part of the walk follows much of the route taken by the legendary Richmond Drummer Boy. At the end of the 18th century, the story says, soldiers in Richmond Castle discovered a tunnel that was thought to lead from there to Easby Abbey. They sent their drummer boy down it, beating his drum so they could follow from above ground. His route went under the Market Square and along to Frenchgate, then beside the river towards the abbey. At the spot now marked by the Drummer Boy Stone, the drumming stopped. The Drummer Boy was never seen again. A version of the story is found in William Maynes's novel *Earthfasts*. The Green Howards Regimental Museum in the Market Square can tell you more about the drummer boy and his regiment.

Abbey and Church

Easby Abbey, whose remains are seen on the walk, was founded for Premonstratensian Canons in 1155 by the Constable of Richmond Castle. Although not much of the church remains, some of the other buildings survive well, including the gatehouse, built about 1300. The refectory is also impressive, and you can see the infirmary, the chapter house and the dormitory. Just by the abbey ruins is the parish church, St Agatha's. It contains a replica of the Anglo-Saxon Easby Cross (the original is in the British Museum) and a set of medieval wall paintings showing Old Testament scenes of Adam and Eve, on the north wall, and the life of Jesus on the south, as well as depictions of activities such as pruning and hawking.

After the abbey, you'll cross the River Swale on the old railway bridge, and follow the track bed. This was part of the branch line from Richmond to Darlington, which opened in 1846. It was closed in 1970. The station has been restored as a cinema and shopping centre, with a café. Look right over Richmond Bridge after you have passed below the castle to see how the stonework differs from one end to the other. It was built by different contractors, one working for Richmond Council and one for the North Riding of Yorkshire. In the hillside below Billy Bank Wood, which you enter beyond the bridge, were copper mines dating back to the 15th century.

RICHMOND

After you have climbed the hill and crossed the 12 stiles (between Points **5** and **6**), you're following the old route of the Swale, which thousands of years ago changed its course and formed the hill known as Round Howe.

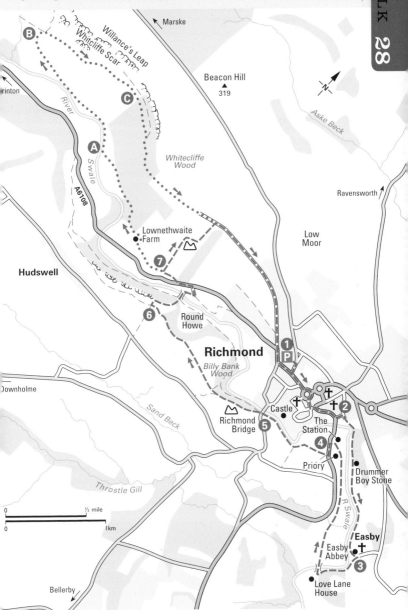

WALK 28 DIRECTIONS

1 Leave the Friars close car park and turn right, then left at the T-junction. At the roundabout, go straight on, down Ryder's Wynd. At the bottom turn left, then go right into Station Road. Just past the church, take Lombards Wynd left.

WALK 28

❷ Turn right at the next junction and follow the track, passing to the right of the Drummer Boy Stone along the path to a gate. Bear right after the gate, still parallel with the river, bearing right again to a gate then along beside the abbey in the village of Easby.

❸ Just beyond the car park turn right, along the track. Follow the wall on the left to Love Lane House. Turn right over the old railway bridge. Follow the track bed, crossing a metalled lane, to the station. Go to the left of the station building to the road.

❹ Turn left, up the road, then turn right up Priory Villas, bearing right to go in front of the houses. Go through three waymarked gates, keeping parallel to the river. Cross some playing fields and pass a clubhouse to a road.

❺ Cross the road and take a signed path opposite, to the left of the cottage. Climb steeply through the woodland, through a gate and straight on to a stile. At the end of

the woodland, bend right, then left to pass a stile in a former crossing fence. Follow the signed path over 12 more stiles. After the last, bear right over another stile, turn left to follow the wall, then go over another stile.

❻ Turn right to go through a gate. Follow the track as it bends downhill, through a gate, to a bridge. Cross it and walk to the lane. Go left and left again at the main road. After 200yds (183m), go right up a bridleway-signed track, to a junction.

❼ Turn right and follow the track uphill, bearing right, then left near the farmhouse, to reach a metalled lane. Turn right and follow the lane back into Richmond. Go ahead at the main road and follow it as it bends left to the garage, where you turn left back to the car park.

WHAT TO LOOK OUT FOR

Wynds are a feature of the Richmond townscape. A northern term, from the Old English word for 'to spiral', these narrow lanes usually link two wider streets. You'll see Friar's Wynd to your right, beside the Georgian Theatre Royal, as you begin the walk, and you'll go down Ryder's Wynd and along Lombard's Wynd. This last was once part of the ancient route up from the banks of the River Swale to the north-eastern area of the town around Frenchgate – 'Frankesgate' in the Middles Ages. Both these names suggest that this part of the town was once occupied by foreign workers; they may have been helping to build the castle. Finkle Street, that runs north-west from the Market Place, has a name that is often found in Yorkshire towns and means 'crooked'. West of the Market Square is Newbiggin, the 'new settlement' – new, that is in 1071 when the castle was begun.

Richmond and the River Swale

To explore the valley of the River Swale a little further, take this loop to Whitcliffe Scar, with a taste of classic Swaledale landscape.
See map and information panel for Walk 28

DISTANCE 9.5 miles (15.3km)   MINIMUM TIME 4hrs
ASCENT/GRADIENT 754ft (230m) ▲▲▲   LEVEL OF DIFFICULTY +++

WALK 29 DIRECTIONS (Walk 28 option)

Richmond is the gateway to the wonderful northern dale of Swaledale. To catch a glimpse of this bewitchingly beautiful landscape you can follow the River Swale a bit further upstream, then climb up to the impressive limestone crags of Whitcliffe Scar.

At Point **7** on the main walk, don't turn right but continue ahead along the track. Just before a farm, follow waymarks to go right to a stile, then follow the hedge to the left to another stile and on to the woodland track. Follow the track to leave the woodland and meet a grassy track, Point **A**.

Turn right and follow the track parallel with the river. Go over two stiles to ascend to a third stile. Pass a barn, go over another stile and bend half right. You are now at the foot of Deep Dale, a dry valley cut by melting water from Ice Age glaciers on the heights rushing down to the valley below. The moorland above you is part of the extensive army training area associated with Catterick Garrison a few miles away.

Go through a gap in the wall, and turn right to a stile by a gate,
Point **B**. Follow the sign straight ahead, then bend right by the ruined wall.

Continue uphill to a stile over a wall, cross the lane and go over another two stiles to turn right on a farm track. Above you is Whitcliffe Scar, from where Robert Willance fell in 1606 when his young horse bolted in the fog. The horse died but he survived, with a broken leg. Knowing that rescue would be some time coming, he slit open the horse's belly and put his leg inside, keeping it warm and preventing gangrene. He lived, and the place became known as Willance's Leap.

A few paces down the track, go left over a stile and follow the track through a gate to a stile by a gate into woodland, Point **C**. Follow the track and leave the woodland by a gate. Continue through two more gateways. The lane becomes metalled and rejoins Walk 28 back into Richmond just beyond Point **7**.

Romantic Hackfall – A Lost Landscape

Walking through a remarkable 18th-century Romantic landscape enjoyed in the 19th and neglected for much of the 20th.

DISTANCE *5.5 miles (8.8km)*   MINIMUM TIME *2hrs 15min*

ASCENT/GRADIENT *623ft (190m)* ▲▲▲   LEVEL OF DIFFICULTY **+++**

PATHS *Woodland paths (muddy at all times), field tracks, 4 stiles*

LANDSCAPE *Artificial Romantic garden, woods, river gorge and fields*

SUGGESTED MAP *OS Explorer 298 Nidderdale*

START/FINISH *Grid reference: SE 230765*

DOG FRIENDLINESS *Dogs can be off lead in woodland*

PARKING *Roadside parking in Grewelthorpe*

PUBLIC TOILETS *None en route*

WALK 30 DIRECTIONS

From the village, walk up the road towards Masham. In 100yds (91m) beyond the speed restriction sign, turn right opposite Hackfall House on a footpath. Cross the bridge and, at the bottom of the steps, turn left to follow the path through the wood. You are now in Hackfall Woods. Once among the most famous of gardens in England, it was painted by Turner, recommended by Wordsworth as a place to visit on the way to the Lake District – and was even depicted on a Wedgwood dinner service owned by Russian Empress Catherine the Great. Laid out in the 1750s by William Aislabie as an antidote to the formality of his father's nearby Studley Royal, the garden attracted visitors right up to the 1920s.

During your walk you will see some of the buildings Aislabie built there, mostly Gothic follies and garden houses, now in disrepair. Hackfall was sold in 1932 to a timber merchant, who felled the beech trees and left the

rest to moulder. Its rescue came about through the Woodland Trust, which now manages it with a light hand and with the support of the local Hackfall Trust.

At a crossing of paths, turn right, downhill. Where the winding path meets a crossing stream, turn right. Just before reaching the octagonal Fisher's Hall, bear right at the fork and go down to the River Ure. This is one of the most spectacular stretches of the river, where it passes through a narrow gorge – a mid-19th-century guidebook spoke of 'the abyss at your feet, where the black waters sleep in cavernous gloom.'

Take the path immediately to the right of steps and follow the path, in places with duckboards

WHERE TO EAT AND DRINK
The Crown Inn in Grewelthorpe, nearly 400 years old, serves home-cooked bar meals and also has a popular restaurant. It prides itself on its real ales. For a wider choice, the city of Ripon is only 20 minutes drive away.

and steps. Just beyond a pair of gateposts, take the middle of three paths, uphill. The path zig-zags up Limehouse Hill, with wide views. Near a wall, turn right of the track through a way-marked gate. Follow the edge of the wood, and soon re-enter at a gate on the right. The path returns to the river bank, then rises to come out of the woods at a signed gate. Go along the raised grassy track to another gate and turn right along the track. Bear right, then left between farm buildings and pass left of a house. Behind it, notice the arched niches in an outbuilding; they once held bee skeps. At the top of the track, turn left along a grassy track and eventually join the road, turning left. Pass a junction and, where the road bends left and the wood starts, go through a gate on the right. Just after the gate, take a grassy path on the left, up through the wood. At a stony track, go left for a few paces, then right to continue uphill. At then next track bend, turn right and after a few paces go left, still uphill, to a track on the ridge. Turn left. After about 200yds (183m), turn right down towards a small gate.

Follow the path beyond half left towards the top of the hill to a stile. Continue ahead to another stile in the hedge on your left. Go diagonally right across the field with a trig point to the left. There are also wide views from here – Roseberry Topping is visible in clear weather. Go over two more stiles, then diagonally to the opposite corner of the field to reach a road through two stone posts. Turn left along the road back to Grewelthorpe, where you might reflect on the 19th-century guidebook's words 'To those who are gladdened by the works of Nature, and a ramble in an umbrageous retreat, there cannot be afforded a richer treat than a trip to Hackfall.'

WHILE YOU'RE THERE

Masham (pronounced Massam) north of Grewelthorpe, has a huge market square and a fine church. It is renowned for its annual sheep fair, but these days many visitors come for the two breweries – Theakston's and Black Sheep. The older, Theakston's, is famous for its Old Peculier beer, named after a legal quirk that meant that Masham had its own 'Peculier' courts, free of interference from the Archbishop of York. The rival Black Sheep Brewery, set up by another of the Theakston family, has equally good ales. Both the breweries have visitor centres.

WHAT TO LOOK OUT FOR

Scattered through the woods at Hackfall are the ornamental buildings, now ruinous, that once formed stopping points on the tour of the gardens. The octagonal Fisher's Hall, dated on a tablet 1750, was built by Aislabie to commemorate his gardener, John Fisher. More substantial are Mowbray Castle, a Gothic sham-ruin tower, subject of a painting by Turner; and Mowbray Point Banqueting House. This is a classical fantasy, now restored as a holiday home by The Landmark Trust, with two distinct faces – one Greek and the other Roman. The servants who waited on the gentry during their banquets had their own Gothic building some distance away. The other buildings, which include a rustic temple made of cyclopean stones, and the Sand Bed Hut, described by one writer as a 'prehistoric folly', are gradually being rescued from the thickets. The Alum Spring and the waterfall have been restored, and the great fountain will one day play again in the circular pool.

A Kingdom for a Horse

*From Middleham Castle, favourite home of King Richard III,
and back via the gallops for today's thoroughbreds.*

WALK 31

DISTANCE *7 miles (11.3km)* MINIMUM TIME *2hrs 30min*

ASCENT/GRADIENT *475ft (145m)* ▲▲ LEVEL OF DIFFICULTY ✦✦✦

PATHS *Field paths and tracks, with some road walking, 14 stiles*

LANDSCAPE *Gentle farmland, riverside paths, views of Wensleydale*

SUGGESTED MAP *OS Explorer OL 30 Yorkshire Dales –
Northern & Central*

START/FINISH *Grid reference: SE 127877*

DOG FRIENDLINESS *Livestock and horses in fields, so dogs on lead*

PARKING *In square in centre of Middleham*

PUBLIC TOILETS *Middleham*

When Richard III died at the battle of Bosworth Field in 1485, Middleham lost one of its favourite residents. Richard had lived here – in the household of the Earl of Warwick –The Kingmaker – when a boy, and set up home here with the Earl's daughter Anne after their marriage. As Duke of Gloucester, it was his power base as effective ruler of the North under his brother Edward IV. Locals don't believe the propagandist version of Richard, promoted by Shakespeare's play, that he was a murderer – the Lord Mayor of York reported to his council after Bosworth that 'King Richard, late lawfully reigning over us, was through great treason piteously slain and murdered.' Middleham Castle today is a splendid ruin, with one of the biggest keeps in England, impressive curtain walls and a deep moat. It is in the care of English Heritage.

From Middleham, the walk takes us to the River Cover and along its banks. After crossing Hullo Bridge the path passes near Braithwaite Hall. Owned by the National Trust and open by appointment only, this is a modest farmhouse of 1667, with three fine gables and unusual oval windows beneath them. Inside are stone-flagged floors, a fine oak staircase and wood panelling, all of the late 17th century. On the hillside behind are the earthworks of a hill-fort, thought to be Iron Age. After the Hall, the lane eventually crosses Coverham Bridge, probably built by the monks of nearby Coverham Abbey. There are a few remains of the abbey, founded in the 12th century, mostly incorporated into later buildings on the site. Miles Coverdale, who was the first man to complete a full English translation of the Bible, came from here.

Middleham – the Lambourne of the North

For many people, Middleham is the home of famous racehorses, and you may be lucky enough to see some in training as you walk over Middleham Low Moor towards the end of the walk – make sure you keep out of their way. More than 500 horses train in Middleham, under the watchful eyes of 13 trainers. Both the Low Moor and the High Moor have been used for exercise for more than 300 years; one of the earliest recorded winners was Bay Bolton, born in 1705, which won Queen Anne's Gold Cup at York Races. Among early jockeys was the splendidly-named 'Crying Jackie' Mangle, who won the St Leger five times in the 1770s and 80s.

To your left as you leave the Low Moor and make your way back to the castle is William's Hill, the remains of the original motte-and-bailey castle built here by the Normans after 1066 to guard the approaches to Wensleydale and Coverdale. The motte, 40ft (12m) high, is joined by a curved bailey surrounded by a ditch. It was abandoned in 1170 when the new castle was begun nearby.

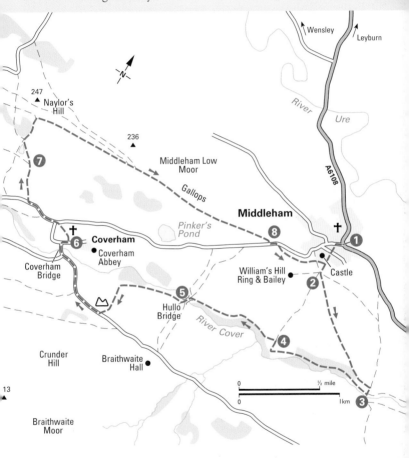

WALK 31 DIRECTIONS

❶ From the square, take the Coverham road then turn left up a passage beside the Castle Keep Tea Rooms. Continue left of Middleham Castle along a walled track to a gate.

❷ Bear left across the big field, following the sign for 'stepping stones'. Cross two more fields, over waymarked stiles. After the third stile, follow the field-edge above a steep bank. At a crossing wall turn right, down to the River Cover by the stepping stones.

❸ Turn right (do not cross the river) and follow the path through woods and a field. A gate leads to steps and an elevated section.

After returning to the river bank, cross a stile into a field. After another stile at its end, turn immediately right. Climb steeply to a marker post.

4 Turn left and follow the edge of a wood. At the end of the field, go left through the trees, then straight ahead on an obvious descending path. Cross a stile and turn left to Hullo Bridge.

WHAT TO LOOK OUT FOR

If you're lucky, you may see the iridescent blue and orange of the kingfisher, fishing above the waters of the River Cover. Vulnerable both to pollution and the ravages of a harsh winter, the kingfisher lives in the banks of the river, digging out a burrow up to 3ft (1m) deep. At the end, a nest is constructed for the female to lay six or seven eggs. Kingfishers catch fish with their fearsome bills and carry them back to their perches overlooking the stream. They carefully turn them so the head faces outwards from the bill, and hit them against the perch to stun or kill them, before swallowing them whole.

5 Cross the bridge and turn right on a permissive path, crossing three stiles. At a crossing wire fence turn left. Cross another stile. Where the fence bends right, go ahead up a steep bank to reach a gate on to a lane. Turn right and descend to Coverham Bridge. Cross the bridge and turn right on a track.

6 Before iron gates, turn left through a small gate, climbing beside a waterfall into the churchyard. Leave by the lychgate and bear left along the main road (signed to Forbidden Corner). After 0.25 mile (400m), go through a gate on the right opposite a disused factory. Bear slightly left, cross three stiles, then

WHILE YOU'RE THERE

Nearby Wensley, after which the dale takes its name, was once a market town, but plague in 1563 reduced it to this little village. Visit the church to see the monumental brass to the priest Simon de Wensley – one of the best in the country – and the wonderful out-of-place Scrope family pew, partly made of the rood screen from Easby Abbey near Richmond.

aim for a prominent gap between buildings and continue through a narrow strip of woodland.

7 Bear slightly left to a stile, right of a stone wall. Skirt ornamental ponds to meet a track. Turn right and ascend past a house to a gateway on to a wider track. Turn right. Where the track bends right, keep straight ahead across the grassy moor; look for occasional blue-topped posts marking the line of a bridleway. When the long fenced gallops appear, keep them to your left and continue down to the road.

8 Turn left. Just before the Middleham sign, take a signposted path on the right. Cross the stile, turn left and follow the path parallel to the road. Go through a stile and a gate, then bear left down to another stile and through a gate on to the lane. Turn left and return to the square.

WHERE TO EAT AND DRINK

Several of Middleham's hotels and inns offer meals and snacks as well as drinks. The White Swan has bar meals and a noted Brasserie, open lunchtime and evenings. The Richard III has a varied bar menu, specialising in sausages. The Castle Keep and The Nosebag are both good, friendly tea rooms.

The Mines of Greenhow and Bewerley Moor

Through a landscape of lead mining, from one of Yorkshire's highest villages.

DISTANCE 6 miles (9.7km)   MINIMUM TIME 2hrs 45min

ASCENT/GRADIENT 1,181ft (360m) ▲▲▲   LEVEL OF DIFFICULTY ✦✦✦

PATHS Field and moorland paths and tracks, 4 stiles

LANDSCAPE Moorland and valley, remains of lead-mining industry

SUGGESTED MAP OS Explorer 298 Nidderdale

START/FINISH Grid reference: SE 128643

DOG FRIENDLINESS Dogs can be off lead for much of route

PARKING Car park at Toft Gate Lime Kiln

PUBLIC TOILETS None en route

It is a long haul from Pateley Bridge up Greenhow Hill to the village of Greenhow, one of the highest in Yorkshire, at around 1,300ft (396m) above sea level. Until the early 17th century this was all bleak and barren moorland. When lead mining on a significant scale developed in the area in the 1600s, a settlement was established here, though most of the surviving buildings are late 18th and 19th century. Many of the cottages also have a small piece of attached farmland, for the miners were also farmers, neither occupation alone giving them a stable income or livelihood. In a way typical of such mining villages, the church and the pub – the Miners Arms, of course – are at the very centre.

Romans and Monks

Romans are the first known miners of Greenhow, though there is said to be some evidence of even earlier activity, as far back as the Bronze Age. The Romans had a camp near Pateley Bridge, and ingots of lead – called 'pigs' – have been found near by, dating from the 1st century AD. In the Middle Ages lead from Yorkshire became important for roofing castles and cathedrals – it is said that it was even used in Jerusalem. Production was governed by the major landowners, the monasteries, and some, like Fountains and Byland, became rich from selling charters for mining and from royalties. After the monasteries were dissolved, the new landowners wanted to exploit their mineral rights, and encouraged many small-scale enterprises in return for a share of the profits.

As you leave Greenhow and begin to descend into the valley of the Gill Beck, you pass through the remains of the Cockhill Mine. It is still possible to make out the dressing floor, where the lead ore was separated from the waste rock and other minerals, and the location of the smelt works, where the ore was processed. Beyond, by the Ashfold Side Beck, were the Merryfield Mines and, where the route crosses the beck, there are extensive remains of the Prosperous Smelt Mill. All these mines were active in the middle of the 19th century, and some had a brief resurgence in the mid 20th.

Besides the Lead

The vast retaining banks of Coldstones Quarry rise above the car park at Toft Gate Lime Kiln. This enormous hole (you can see it from the viewing point at the top of the bank) opened about 1900 and produces almost 1 million tons of limestone a year. Around Greenhow, the limestone layers are particularly deep, allowing large blocks to be cut. Across it run two mineral veins, called Garnet Vein and Sun Vein, both of which have been mined for lead and for fluorite. Other minerals found in smaller quantities in the rock here are barite, calcite and galena, as well as crystals of cerrusite, anglesite and occasionally quartz.

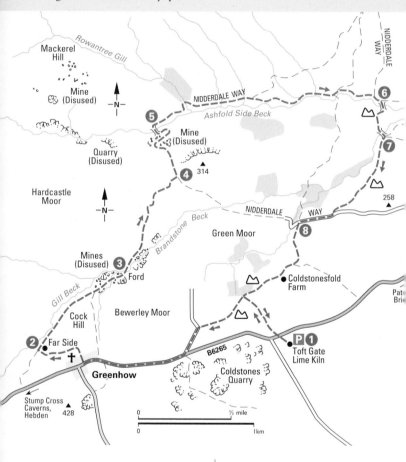

WALK 32 DIRECTIONS

❶ Cross the road from the car park and go over the stile opposite into a field. Follow the faint path downhill to a gate. Descend bearing left, passing above a barn. Cross another stile and descend to a metalled track. Turn left and walk up the hill to a road.

Turn left and walk up to the main road. Turn right and follow this down into Greenhow village. At the bottom of the hill, just past a converted chapel, take a lane to the right. At the junction go left and follow the lane to a cattle grid. Follow waymarks along the wire fence, round to the right to pass behind the house (Far Side).

2 Follow the track past Low Far Side and down into the valley of Gill Beck and then Brandstone Beck, where there are the extensive remains of lead mining activity. Where the track swings left, keep straight on down through the scars and spoil heaps to meet another track at a ford.

WHILE YOU'RE THERE

The limestone cave system at nearby Stump Cross Caverns was discovered in the middle of the 19th century. You can visit a succession of caves with plenty of stalagmites and stalactites, many with fanciful names, where ancient animal bones, including those of the wolverine, have been discovered. It is open daily from mid-March to mid-November.

3 Cross and follow the obvious track up the hill. Go over a stile beside a gate by trees then, 100yds (91m) beyond, take another stile on the right. Follow the track towards a house but before reaching it, turn left between stone walls and descend to another stile and T-junction with another track.

4 Turn left and go through a waymarked gateway. Descend to spoil heaps, then follow steep paths downhill just to the right of the heaps. Turn left by an iron cogwheel to a footbridge over Ashfold Side Beck.

WHAT TO LOOK OUT FOR

The lime kiln at Toft Gate is very well-preserved and is now protected by English Heritage. It was built in the 1860s to help meet the Victorians' huge demand for lime, both in agriculture and building. A path from the car park leads you round the site where the flue, chimney and main furnace are visible. You can also see inside the kiln itself and interpretive panels explain the workings.

5 Follow the path slanting up to the right to meet a track. Follow this down the valley, eventually going through a series of caravan sites. About one mile (1.6km) from the footbridge, the Nidderdale Way leaves the track at a signpost. Go straight on for another 100yds (91m), then turn right through a metal gate near a toilet block and then over a bridge.

6 Climb the steep track away from the river and, as the gradient eases, go left on a green track between stone walls. Nearing a house, go right a few paces then cross a footbridge.

WHERE TO EAT AND DRINK

Sadly, the Miners Arms in Greenhow has closed, so either head west to Stump Cross Caverns and its tea room or east to Pateley Bridge, which is well served with hotels, pubs, restaurants and tea rooms. Apothecary's House serves light lunches and teas. Grassfields Country House Hotel in Low Wath Road has both a restaurant and a bistro in an elegant Georgian mansion.

7 Turn right through a gate and follow the rough track uphill. Meet another track at a T-junction and turn left, but as the track begins to bend left, bear right across the grass to a kissing gate and a metalled lane. Turn right.

8 About 100yds (91m) after passing Low Waite Farm on the right, fork left on a track. Just before a cattle grid, turn right and follow the rougher track up to Coldstonesfold Farm. Continue along the metalled track to a waymarked post on a bend, where you turn left to retrace your outward route to return to Toft Gate Lime Kiln.

Around Reeth in the Heart of Swaledale

Farmers, miners, knitters and nuns all played their part in the history of this part of Swaledale.

DISTANCE 5.5 miles (8.8km)   MINIMUM TIME 2hrs

ASCENT/GRADIENT 508ft (155m) ▲▲▲   LEVEL OF DIFFICULTY ✦✦✦

PATHS Field and riverside paths, lanes and woodland, 14 stiles

LANDSCAPE Junction of Swaledale and Arkengarthdale, with field and surrounding moorland

SUGGESTED MAP OS Explorer OL 30 Yorkshire Dales – Northern & Central

START/FINISH Grid reference: SE 039993

DOG FRIENDLINESS Dogs should be on lead for majority of walk

PARKING In Reeth, behind fire station, or by the Green (voluntary payment requested)

PUBLIC TOILETS Reeth, near Buck Hotel

Reeth has always had a strategic role in the Yorkshire Dales. Set above the junction of Swaledale and Arkengarthdale on Mount Calva, it controlled the important route westwards from Richmond. Sheep were, for a long time, the basis of Reeth's prosperity – it has been a market town since 1695 – and there are still annual sheep sales each autumn, as well as the important Reeth Show around the beginning of September. The wool was used in Reeth's important knitting industry – both the men and women would click away with their needles at stockings and other garments. Reeth also used to be a centre for the lead-mining industry, which extended up Arkengarthdale and over Marrick Moor.

Two Bridges and a Church

Reeth Bridge, reached by the Leyburn road from the Green, has suffered over the years from the effects of the swollen River Swale. The present bridge dates from the early 18th century, replacing one washed away in 1701, itself built after its predecessor succumbed in 1547. The path beside the river takes us to Grinton Bridge. Nearby is Grinton church, once the centre of a huge parish that took in the whole of Swaledale, making very long journeys necessary for marriages and funerals. Curiously, it began life as a mission church for the Augustinian canons of far-away Bridlington Priory on the east coast.

Nuns and Schools at Marrick

The approach to Marrick Priory along the lane suggests that you are about to reach one of the most important churches in the Dales. In a way that is true. Marrick in the Middle Ages was home to a group of Benedictine nuns. It was founded by Roger de Aske, whose descendent, Robert, was one of the leaders of the Pilgrimage of Grace, the uprising against King Henry VIII's closure of the monasteries. Hilda Prescott's novel *The Man on a Donkey*, about Robert Aske and the Pilgrimage, is partly set at Marrick.

Today the nuns' buildings are partly demolished or absorbed into farm buildings. The church was reduced in size in 1811, and the complex is now used as a Youth Centre for the Diocese of Ripon and Leeds, offering outdoor sports and adventure training.

After Marrick Priory the path climbs steeply uphill on rough stone steps called the Nun's Causey (a corruption of causeway). Now used as part of the Coast to Coast Walk, from St Bee's Head in Cumbria to Robin Hood's Bay on the east coast, this is said to be the route which the nuns from the priory built so they could reach the old Richmond road that ran along the summit of the hill. The original 365 steps have been broken up and removed over the centuries, but the path still retains a suitably medieval atmosphere.

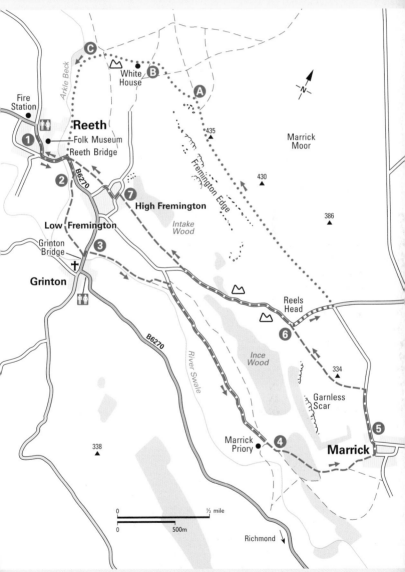

WALK 33 DIRECTIONS

❶ From the Green, walk downhill, in the direction of Leyburn, to Reeth Bridge. Over the bridge, continue along the road as it swings right. About 100yds (91m) along, turn right at a footpath sign to Grinton.

❷ Follow the riverside path to a signpost, then continue on a well-marked path across fields to ascend steps on to Grinton Bridge. Turn left a few paces, cross the road and take a track beside the bridge.

❸ Follow the riverside path for about 0.5 mile (800m) to a metalled lane. Turn right and follow the lane to Marrick Priory. Walk past the buildings, over a cattle grid, and bear left through a gate signed 'Marrick'.

❹ Walk up the grassy track, then follow the paved path through woodland. Continue through fields, with a wall on the right, on to a metalled lane. Opposite Harlands House turn left, then left again at a triangular junction.

❺ Follow the road for 0.25 mile (400m), and turn left over a stile at a footpath sign. Follow the wall, crossing to the other side at a waymarked stile. Continue along the wall then keep on in the same direction, descending slightly to meet a road.

❻ Turn left and follow the road for 0.75 mile (1.2km). On a left bend near an obvious track to a farm, cross a stile on the right, signed 'Fremington'. Go straight ahead to a stile then continue along the well-marked path through fields, until a final gate leads on to a walled path behind houses. Go straight ahead to a lane.

❼ Turn left then first right. As the lane bends left, go ahead to a stile by a gate. Keep by the wall on the left, and follow the path through more stiles back to Reeth Bridge. Cross the bridge and follow the road back to the Green.

WHAT TO LOOK OUT FOR
Traditionally, Dales farmers had their own way of counting their sheep, starting (from one) yahn, tayhn, tether, mether, mimp, hither, lither, anver, danver...and wherever you go in this area you are likely to come across the Swaledale sheep. This hardy breed, which spends much of its life out in the open on exposed moorland, has thick wool that is very resistant to wet. When spun it is very hardwearing, and modern treatment methods ensure that any harshness is removed. This didn't seem to have worried the Swaledale knitters, who from the time of Queen Elizabeth I onwards used the wool in their products. She encouraged the production of woollen stockings, and Swaledale's first pair was presented to her. By the 18th century 18,000 pairs, all hand knitted, were being produced annually.

From Reeth up to Fremington Edge

For wide views of Swaledale and Arkengarthdale, take this extra section, which takes you up on to Fremington Edge.
See map and information panel for Walk 33

DISTANCE *7 miles (11.3km)*   **MINIMUM TIME** *3hrs*
ASCENT/GRADIENT *328ft (100m)* ▲▲▲   **LEVEL OF DIFFICULTY** ✦✦✦

WALK 34 DIRECTIONS
(Walk 33 option)

You can extend your walk in the heart of Swaledale by climbing up to the moors of Fremington Edge.

At Point **6** on the main walk turn right, uphill. By the road sign to Marrick, go left through a stile. Go straight across a field then follow a wall on the left. The track becomes clearer as it reaches heather moorland, climbing gently over Fremington Edge, with superb views of Swaledale.

All around are dry-stone walls, some reaching in long, straight lines to the summit of the moors. These were built to enclose land after the Parliamentary Enclosure Act of 1778. Such enclosure was recommended by Sir Thomas Elliot of Fremington, responsible for the improvement of much of Yorkshire's moorland. As the track starts to descend, you pass an area of spoil heaps. Just beyond is a gate on the left, Point **A**.

Go through the gate and follow a faint path half right. Reeth appears dramatically below. Bear right along the brink of a very steep slope (beware broken crags below), then slant down to a gap in a wall. Continue the slanting descent through the remains of chert mines. Chert, a hard flint-like black or white stone, was used, finely ground, in the pottery industry. You reach a track near a footpath sign, Point **B**. From the sign, follow a grassy path above White House to a gated stile. Bear left on a green path, soon descending steeply to a track, signpost and stile, Point **C**.

WHERE TO EAT AND DRINK

All three of Reeth's pubs – The King's Arms and the Black Bull (next door to each other) and the Buck Inn – provide good food at lunchtime and in the evenings. The Black Bull is particularly noted for its pies. There are also tea rooms and cafés around the Green.

Cross the stile, walk past a barn and through two more stiles, then bear left, parallel with the river, with a wall on your left. Go through a stile, pass a barn, then through the left of two gates in a crossing wall. Continue through a long narrow field to the road by Reeth Bridge, rejoining the main walk. Cross the bridge to return to the Green.

River and Woodland at Bolton Abbey

Over moorland and alongside the Strid to the ruined priory.

DISTANCE 6.75 miles (10.9km)   MINIMUM TIME 2hrs 30min

ASCENT/GRADIENT 870ft (265m) ▲▲▲   LEVEL OF DIFFICULTY +++

PATHS Field and moorland paths, then level riverside paths, 3 stiles

LANDSCAPE Moorland with wide views and riverside woodland

SUGGESTED MAP OS Explorer OL 2 Yorkshire Dales – Southern & Western

START/FINISH Grid reference: SE 071539

DOG FRIENDLINESS Must be on lead in woodland and on moorland

PARKING Main pay-and-display car park at Bolton Abbey

PUBLIC TOILETS By car park and at Cavendish Pavilion

WALK 35 DIRECTIONS

Leave the car park at its north end, by the Village Store. Turn right and walk to the B6160. Turn left and follow the road under an arch, an aqueduct built in the 18th century to carry water to a mill, to reach the battlemented Bolton Hall, originally the gateway to Bolton Priory (it was never an abbey), and later a hunting lodge for the Earls of Cumberland and their successors the Dukes of Devonshire, who still own the estate.

Opposite Bolton Hall turn left on a signed track. At the top of the track, go through a gate on the right, with a bridleway sign. Walk under a power line to a signpost. Go past pools to a gate, then bear right to another gate into woodland. Follow the rising track through the wood, with several signs, to another gate. Follow blue waymarks, most painted on rocks, across fields. At a crest, bear left to a gate in a corner, then turn left along the wall. The path climbs more steeply on to Hare Head, which has wide views. Descend

gently to a gate, and 20yds (18m) beyond, take a path downhill, trending right lower down, to a signpost. Turn right, parallel to the road, to another signpost 'FP to B6160'. Follow the track to a stile, then take the left fork, going roughly level across the moor, to a wall-corner. Continue to the next wall, then turn right along it, following an improving track to a signpost.

Go left over a stile and straight down to the road. Turn right a few paces then enter the car park. Pass the Strid Wood Visitor Centre.

WHILE YOU'RE THERE

Take a trip on the Embsay and Bolton Abbey Steam Railway, which has a station 1.5 miles (2.4km) south of the priory. Operated by enthusiasts, the railway runs steam trains at weekends, and on most days in August; at other times there is a historic diesel service. At Christmas and on other special days there are themed rides, and the railway also holds regular Thomas the Tank Engine Days.

BOLTON ABBEY

Here you can learn about the birds and plants of the Strid Woods, which are open to the public and well way-marked. Follow tracks down to the river bank, signposted to the Strid. Here, the River Wharfe thunders through a narrow cleft between rocks, the Strid itself, a place loved by the Victorians. The flow is fast and the river is 30ft (9m) deep, so don't be tempted to cross; there have been many drownings over the years. Continue along the easy riverside track to reach an information board and gateway near the Cavendish Pavilion café. A survivor from the first years of the 20th century, the Pavilion has been restored and added to over the years.

Bear left by the café and cross the footbridge. Turn right immediately, signed 'Bolton Abbey'. The path briefly joins a vehicle track to cross a side stream, then leaves again, bearing right. When this path forks, either branch will do but the higher probably has better views of the priory. Descend to a bridge beside stepping stones over the river near the priory. This was built for Augustinian canons who founded their house here in 1154. The ruins make one of the most romantic scenes in the country, and many great English artists, including Girtin and Turner, have painted it. Much of what remains was complete by 1220; the last prior, unaware of the coming storm that would sweep away monastic life, began a tower at the west end. It remained unfinished when the monasteries were suppressed. Most of the buildings fell gradually into ruin, but the nave of the priory church was given to the local people, and it is still their parish church. Cross the bridge and walk straight ahead. Climb steps to a gateway – the Hole in the Wall. Go through to the road, left a few paces, then turn right to return to the car park.

WHAT TO LOOK OUT FOR

The priory church is worth exploring carefully. It is a fascinating mix of Norman and later styles – look out for the tell-tale round Norman arches and the pointed arches of the later work. The west front is very complicated – particularly because of the tower added just before the priory was shut. This has a huge, decorative window, but masks an even better 13th-century west front. The eastern end of the church, where the canons worshipped, is in ruins. The remains of the huge east window are among the most memorable things about Bolton Priory. The nave, now the parish church, still gives an impression of the building's original grandeur. Notice the stained-glass windows on the right-hand side as you enter. They date from the first half of the 19th century and were designed, in convincing medieval style, by Augustus Pugin, whose decorative work is found everywhere in the Houses of Parliament.

Scar House
and Nidderdale

A walk in Upper Nidderdale,
with natural and artificial landscapes.

DISTANCE **8.5 miles (13.7km)**   MINIMUM TIME **3hrs 45min**

ASCENT/GRADIENT **1,050ft (320m) ▲▲▲**   LEVEL OF DIFFICULTY **+++**

PATHS **Moorland tracks, field paths and lanes, 11 stiles**

LANDSCAPE **High hills of Upper Nidderdale, farmland and riverside**

SUGGESTED MAP **OS Explorer 298 Nidderdale or OS Explorer OL 30 Yorkshire Dales – Northern & Central**

START/FINISH **Grid reference: SE 070766**

DOG FRIENDLINESS **Can be off lead on moorland, on lead in farmland**

PARKING **Signed car park at top of reservoir access road**

PUBLIC TOILETS **By car park**

Opened in 1936, Scar House is one of a string of reservoirs in Nidderdale that serve the city of Bradford, 30 miles (48km) to the south – the others include Angram, to the west, and Gouthwaite, down the valley towards Pateley Bridge. It is still possible to see evidence around the dam of the remains of the village in which the navvies who built it lived and of the ancillary buildings where they stored machinery and dressed the stone. There were some protests before the dams were built about the drowning of parts of the valley, and rumours that Nidderdale was left out of the Yorkshire Dales National Park when it was designated in 1954 because the reservoirs had blighted the landscape. Redress was made in 1994 when 603 square miles (1,562sq km) of Nidderdale became an Area of Outstanding Natural Beauty.

How Stean Gorge

'Yorkshire's Little Switzerland' says the publicity for How Stean Gorge. The How Stean Beck has forced its way through the limestone here, cutting a gorge up to 80ft (25m) deep, with pools and overhangs enough to please both geologists and small children. For a fee, you can enter the gorge, crossing and re-crossing by footbridges and exploring the narrow paths. The more adventurous can borrow a torch to investigate the deep Tom Taylor's Cave, said to be named after a highwayman who holed up here.

The village of Middlesmoor, visible after passing How Stean Gorge, is one of the most dramatically sited in the area. Set high on a bluff of the hills overlooking the Nidd Valley, its 19th-century church is on the site of a building thought to have been founded by St Chad; it contains the head of a Saxon Cross. One of the most notorious of Victorian murderers, Eugene Aram, who killed his wife's lover and was hanged when the body came to light 14 years later, was married here. Following the Nidderdale Way from Lofthouse, you may well see groups donning caving gear. They are likely to be preparing to enter the Goyden Pot system, 3.5 miles (5.7km) of underground caves and passages cut through the limestone by the River Nidd. An early guide book noted that 'Goyden Pot Hole is a large Rock, into which the River Nidd enters by an arch finely formed…with a lighted candle a person may walk three hundred yards into it with safety.' This procedure is not recommended today!

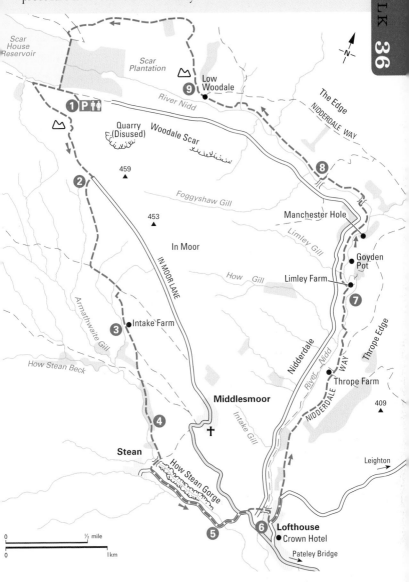

WALK 36 DIRECTIONS

1 Walk past the dam and along the side of the reservoir to a Nidderdale Way signpost. Turn sharp left. The stony track climbs below crags then zig-zags up to open moor. Continue to a gate.

A few paces beyond, go right through another gate.

2 Follow a path down to a wall and bear left. Follow sheep tracks through heather, roughly parallel to the wall, to a track. Turn left, cross two cattle grids, then turn right,

105

down to a gate. Walk down the field to a gate just right of a house.

❸ Descend to a gate left of a ruined barn. Bear right through a gateway then bear left to pass right of another barn. Continue in the same direction into woodland. A clearer path joins from the right; continue ahead, slanting down to the riverside.

❹ Follow the path above the river, then through a field to a lime kiln. Bear left to a ladder stile then follow the edge of woodland to a gate and Nidderdale Way sign. Turn right down steps to cross a footbridge over the river. Follow the path to a lane and go left, passing How Stean Gorge entrance, to a stone bridge.

❺ Follow the lane over the bridge to a T-junction and turn right. At a lay-by on a bend go through a kissing gate. Follow the path beside a cricket ground. Cross a lane and go over a bridge. Bear right and pass between buildings into Lofthouse.

❻ Turn left uphill. As the road bends right, go left on a level grassy track. Ignore branches to the right and follow the main track to Thrope Farm. Keep straight ahead until a waymarked sunken path slants down to the river. Walk upstream then cross to a waymarked gate. Follow a path above the river then join a track towards a farm.

❼ Pass metal sheds, then bear left to a gate beside a house. Follow the track to the river bank and continue upstream, passing Goyden Pot (obvious) and Manchester Hole (in the far bank). Eventually you reach a footbridge over the river. Cross, turn left and continue along the riverside. At New Houses go through a gate, cross a lane and continue along the riverside track.

❽ Where the track bends right, go ahead through stone stiles and continue to a wooden stile. Climb slightly, then bear left to a gate. Descend to another gate, then bear right to a farm. Go ahead between the buildings to a track which climbs and bends right to pass another house.

❾ Climb to a gap between high walls. Continue uphill, with a broken wall on your right, to a gate. Go half left through bracken, to a clear track. Turn left, passing a plantation, and follow the track until it crosses another track, directly above the dam. Descend to the dam and cross it to return back to the car park.

Villages, Falls and Intriguing Follies

From West Burton to Aysgarth and back, via the famous Aysgarth Falls and some unusual farm buildings.

DISTANCE *4 miles (6.4km)* MINIMUM TIME *1hr 30min*

ASCENT/GRADIENT *394ft (120m)* ▲▲▲ LEVEL OF DIFFICULTY +++

PATHS *Field and riverside paths and tracks, 35 stiles*

LANDSCAPE *Two typical Dales villages, fields and falls on the River Ure*

SUGGESTED MAP *OS Explorer OL 30 Yorkshire Dales – Northern & Central*

START/FINISH *Grid reference: SE 017867*

DOG FRIENDLINESS *Dogs should be on lead*

PARKING *Centre of West Burton, by (but not on) the Green*

PUBLIC TOILETS *None en route; Aysgarth National Park visitor centre is close*

Many people regard West Burton as the prettiest village in the Dales. Its wide, irregular green, with a fat obelisk of 1820, is surrounded by small stone cottages, formerly homes to the quarrymen and miners of the district – but no church. Villagers had to make the trek to Aysgarth for services. West Burton has always been an important centre. It is at the entrance to Bishopdale, with its road link to Wharfedale. South is the road to Walden Head, now a dead end for motorists, but for walkers an alternative route to Starbotton and Kettlewell. At the end of the walk you'll travel for a short time, near Flanders Hall, along Morpeth Gate, the old packhorse route to Middleham.

Two Halves of Aysgarth

After crossing the wide flood plain of Bishopdale Beck, and crossing Eshington Bridge, you climb across the hill to descend into Aysgarth. A village of two halves, the larger part, which you come to first, is set along the main A684 road. The walk takes you along the traditional field path from this part of the village to its other half, set around St Andrew's Church. It's worth looking inside; it contains the spectacular choir screen brought here from Jervaulx Abbey, down the dale, when it was closed by Henry VIII. Like the elaborate stall beside it, it was carved by the renowned Ripon workshops.

The Falls and the Wood

Beyond the church, the path follows the river beside Aysgarth's Middle and Lower Falls. The falls were formed by the Ure eating away at the underlying limestone as it descends from Upper Wensleydale to join the deeper Bishopdale. They are now one of the most popular tourist sights in the Yorkshire Dales National Park and the Upper Falls, by the bridge, featured in the film *Robin Hood, Prince of Thieves*. Robin (Kevin Costner) and Little John fought here with long staves.

Mrs Sykes' Follies

On the return leg of the walk, you pass below two oddities in the parkland behind the house at Sorrellsykes Park. These two follies were built in the 18th century by Mrs Sykes and no one seems to knows why. One is a round tower, with a narrowing waist like a diabolo. The other, sitting like Thunderbird 3 ready for lift-off, is known to local people as the 'Rocket Ship'. It is of no practical use, except for minimal shelter in the square room in its base, but it is just one of many folly cones throughout Britain. None of the others, however, have this elaborate arrangement of fins — presumably added because the builder had doubts about its stability.

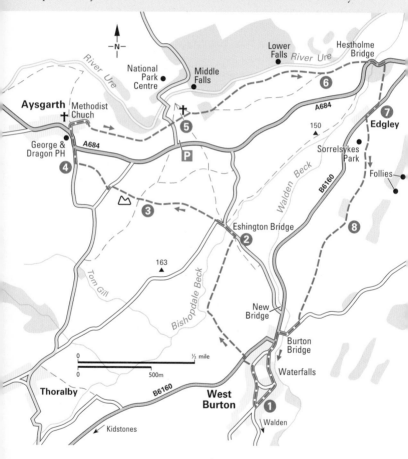

WALK 37 DIRECTIONS

❶ Leave the Green near the Village Shop. Opposite 'Meadowcroft' go left, signed 'Eshington Bridge'. Cross the road, turn right then left, through a gate and down steps. Go through a gate beside a barn, and continue to a stile at the bottom right of the field. Cross two more stiles then bear right to meet a stone wall. Follow this then continue in the same direction to a road.

❷ Turn left, cross the bridge and go up a narrow lane to a bend. Go ahead through a stile, signed 'Aysgarth'. Climb past another stile and left of a barn. Continue up the

WEST BURTON

field and bear left to a gate near the corner, then diagonally across the next field. Keep left of an obvious wall gap to a stile by another gap. Descend to a stile and footpath sign.

❸ Continue in the same direction and up to a signpost. Follow the Aysgarth direction to a gateway and stile. Cross the field half left to a stile on to a lane. Turn left, then right, signed 'Aysgarth'. Go through three stiles to a road.

❹ Turn right, into the village. Go past the George and Dragon then straight ahead to the Methodist Church and bear right along the lane. Cross a stile by Field House. Follow the wall and continue along a short track, then follow a path through eight stiles to a road.

❺ Enter the churchyard, pass right of the church and leave by a stile. Cross a field and go through a wood. Follow the path downhill, descending steps to the river bank. Take a signed stile right.

❻ Follow the path by the river to a signpost. Bend right across a field to the main road. Turn left, cross a bridge, then turn right into woodland, signed 'Edgley', soon bearing left, uphill, to a stile. Bear right across a field to a gate in the far corner and join a road.

❼ Turn right. About 150yds (137m) along, go left over a stile, signed 'Flanders Hall'. Walk towards the follies, then bear right just below the ridge, passing Sorrelsykes Park to your right. Cross a track and bear left past a waymark to a signpost. Turn right to a stepped stone stile, then follow the bottom edge of the field to a gate opposite a stone barn.

❽ Descend through this and two more gates, then bear left along the field-edge to a stile. Continue ahead to a lane. Turn right, cross a bridge and join the village road. Turn left, back to the Green.

WHILE YOU'RE THERE
Visit the Yorkshire Carriage Museum by the bridge below the church in Aysgarth. Its fascinating display of old-time transport, (including carriages, carts, hearses and fire engines) is housed in a former cotton mill that wove cloth for Garibaldi's revolutionary army of 19th-century Italy.

WHAT TO LOOK OUT FOR
The woods around Aysgarth have long been used for the production of hazel poles. Now-overgrown stumps of hazel trees sprouting many branches, some of them of considerable age, are evidence of this trade. In Freeholders' Wood beside the Middle and Lower Falls, across the River Ure from the route of the walk, the National Park Authority has restarted this ancient craft of coppicing. Each year the hazel trees are cut back to a stump – called a stool – from which new shoots are allowed to grow. As long as they are protected from grazing cattle, the shoots develop into poles, and can be harvested after around seven years' growth. Hazel poles are traditionally used for making woven hurdles, and the thinner stems for basket-weaving.

Dalesfolk Traditions in Hubberholme

From JB Priestley's favourite Dales village,
along Langstrothdale and back via a limestone terrace.

DISTANCE 5.25 miles (8.4km) **MINIMUM TIME** 2hrs

ASCENT/GRADIENT 480ft (146m) ▲▲▲ **LEVEL OF DIFFICULTY** +++

PATHS Field paths and tracks, steep after Yockenthwaite, 11 stiles

LANDSCAPE Streamside paths and limestone terrace

SUGGESTED MAP OS Explorer OL 30 Yorkshire Dales – Northern & Central

START/FINISH Grid reference: SD 927782

DOG FRIENDLINESS Dogs should be on lead, except on section between Yockenthwaite and Cray

PARKING Beside river in village, opposite church (not church parking)

PUBLIC TOILETS None en route

Literary pilgrims visit Hubberholme to see the George Inn, where JB Priestley could often be found enjoying the local ale, and the churchyard, the last resting place for his ashes, as he requested. He chose an idyllic spot. Set at the foot of Langstrothdale, Hubberholme is a cluster of old farmhouses and cottages surrounding the church. Norman in origin, St Michael's was once flooded so badly that fish were seen swimming in the nave. One vicar of Hubberholme is said to have carelessly baptised a child Amorous instead of Ambrose, a mistake that, once entered in the parish register, couldn't be altered. Amorous Stanley used his memorable name later in life as part of his stock-in-trade as a hawker.

Church Wood

Hubberholme church's best treasures are of wood. The rood loft above the screen is one of only two surviving in Yorkshire, (the other is at Flamborough, far away on the east coast). Once holding figures of Christ on the Cross, St Mary and St John, it dates from 1558, when such examples of Popery were fast going out of fashion. It still retains some of its once-garish colouring of red, gold and black. Master-carver Robert Thompson provided almost all the rest of the furniture in 1934 – look for his mouse trademark on each piece.

Ancient Yockenthwaite and Remote Cray

Yockenthwaite's name, said to have been derived from an ancient Irish name, Eogan, conjures up images of the ancient past. Norse settlers were here more than 1,000 years ago – and even earlier settlers have left their mark, a Bronze Age stone circle a little further up the valley. The hamlet now consists of a few farm buildings beside the bridge over the Wharfe at the end of Langstrothdale Chase, a Norman hunting ground which used to have its own forest laws and punishments. You walk along a typical Dales limestone terrace to reach Cray, on the road over from Bishopdale joining Wharfedale to Wensleydale. Here is another huddle of farmhouses, around

HUBBERHOLME

the White Lion Inn. You then follow the Cray Gill downstream, past a series of small cascades. For a more spectacular waterfall, head up the road from the inn a little way to Cray High Bridge.

Burning the Candle

Back in Hubberholme, the George Inn was once the vicarage. It is the scene each New Year's Day of an ancient auction. It begins with the lighting of a candle, after which the auctioneer asks for bids for the year's tenancy of the 'Poor Pasture', a 16-acre (6.5ha) field behind the inn. All bids have to be completed before the candle burns out. In the days when the George housed the vicar, he ran the auction. Today a local auctioneer takes the role, and a merry time is had by all. The proceeds from the auction go to help the old people of the village.

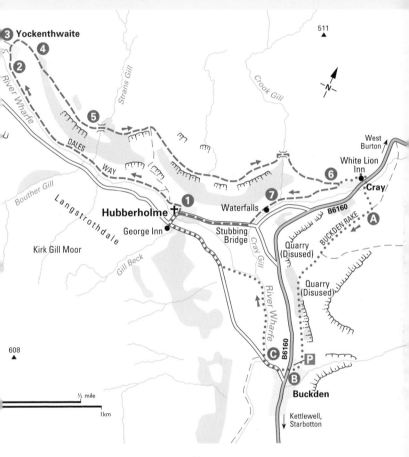

WALK 38 DIRECTIONS

1 Enter the farmyard beside the church and turn left immediately through a Dales Way signed gate. Take the lower path, signed 'Yockenthwaite', alongside the churchyard. Walk beside the river for 1.25 miles (2km); the clear Dales Way path is never far from the river. Approaching Yockenthwaite, go up steps to a little gate and left to a gate and signpost.

2 Follow the track towards a bridge but, before reaching it, go sharp right up a farm track, which swings back left to a sign to Cray and Hubberholme.

3 Go up to another signpost, then follow the obvious track slanting right and up. Part-way up the hill, go right at a footpath sign through a gate.

4 Follow the near-level path to a signpost, then bear left and up a rough section to another signpost. Turn right and follow the obvious path, descending very gently along a beautiful natural terrace until the path goes left and up to enter a wood by a footbridge over a miniature gorge.

5 Walk through the wood then continue, level again, to reach a small side valley above a house. A signpost above the house points towards Cray. Go up slightly, over rocks, then along another green terrace path for about a mile (1.6km) to a footbridge. Cross this, then ascend slightly to a barn; bear right to a gate then follow a marked path across meadow land. Go past a house to a junction of tracks on the edge of Cray.

6 Go sharp right, down to a footpath sign to Stubbing Bridge. Descend between stone walls and through a gate and on to the grassy hillside. Pass another footpath sign and continue downhill to meet the stream.

7 Follow the streamside path past waterfalls and pools, crossing a stone bridge over a side-stream. Cross a stile and continue past a barn to reach the road. Turn right back to the parking place in Hubberholme.

Down the Dale from Cray to Buckden

Take this easy additional loop via a Roman road to Buckden, and back to Hubberholme along the riverside.
See map and information panel for Walk 38

DISTANCE 6.75 miles (10.9km)   MINIMUM TIME 2hrs 30mins
ASCENT/GRADIENT 623ft (190m) ▲▲▲   LEVEL OF DIFFICULTY ✦✦✦

WALK 39 DIRECTIONS
(Walk 38 option)

You can see more of the beautiful Upper Wharfedale scenery by extending Walk 38 from Cray to the peaceful village of Buckden.

At Point ❻ on the main walk, continue straight ahead along the higher track, past farm buildings, to reach a metalled road by the White Lion Inn.

Cross the road and the pub car park to stepping stones. Go through a gate, then fork left to a signpost and go round left, following a wall. Follow the path when it slants away right to a gate, just beyond which is a signpost to Buckden, Point ❹.

Turn right along the level green track. You are now on Buckden Rake, possibly the remains of a Roman road built by the army of Julius Agricola to link the fort at Ilkley in Wharfedale (possibly the Roman outpost of

Olicana) to Virosidum (Bainbridge in Wensleydale). The track eventually becomes stony as it starts to descend, then runs through woodland and into open fields again.

Descend into Buckden car park and go straight ahead by the 'No Exit' sign on to the main road by Town Head Barn, a National Trust property, Point ❸.

Buckden, always a strategically important point in the Dales, is an attractive estate village at the junction of several roads and tracks. It was a centre from which the Norman and medieval noblemen set out to hunt deer in the Langstrothdale Forest; the Buck Inn is a reminder of this tradition. The village is dominated by Buckden Pike, 2,304ft (702m) high, to the north-east. Cross the road and follow the track beside the Green. Turn right along the road and over the bridge. A few paces beyond, follow the Dales Way through a gate on the right, signed 'Hubberholme', Point ❸.

Follow the very clear path, eventually swinging away from the riverside to rejoin the road. Turn right back to Hubberholme, turning right over the bridge back to the church and the car parking place.

The Lead Mines at Old Gang

Ruined buildings give eloquent testimony to Swaledale's important industrial past.

DISTANCE 7.75 miles (12.5km)	**MINIMUM TIME** 3hrs

ASCENT/GRADIENT 853ft (260m) ▲▲▲   **LEVEL OF DIFFICULTY** ✦✦✦

PATHS Tracks and moorland paths – a little road walking at end

LANDSCAPE Pasture and moorland

SUGGESTED MAP OS Explorer OL 30 Yorkshire Dales – Northern & Central

START/FINISH Grid reference: SD 989999

DOG FRIENDLINESS Many grouse, so dogs on lead throughout

PARKING At road junction above Surrender Bridge, in valley of Old Gang Beck

PUBLIC TOILETS None en route

WALK 40 DIRECTIONS

From the parking place, descend to cross the bridge. Climb a little way up the other side, then turn left on a track by a 'BW only, no vehicles' sign. Follow the track for a mile (1.6km) to Old Gang Smelting Mills.

The area around Old Gang was one of the most intensively mined parts of Swaledale in the 18th and 19th centuries. The lead-bearing veins here were very complex, so there are many – and confusing

WHILE YOU'RE THERE

Further your knowledge of the district's lead mining by visiting Gunnerside. The valley of Gunnerside Gill, which stretched north from the village, was one of the most heavily mined areas in Swaledale. A stroll up the valley will enable you to see mine entrances and the remains of crushing mills. There is a particularly impressive show at the Bunton site, where the valley is steep, while beyond are the ruins of the Blakethwaite Smelting Mill.

– remains. The largest surviving building beside the track at Old Gang is the smelting mill, while on the hillside above is a long row of stone columns, the remains of the peat house. This open-sided building, 390ft (119m) long and 21ft (6.4m) wide, originally had a thatched roof. It could hold enough locally dug peat to fuel a year's smelting. Continue along the track, passing the entrance to Hard Level, opened in 1785. Look back from the first rise for the best view of the peat-house columns. Keep right where the track forks, following the Level House Bridge sign. Level House was a dwelling built in the late 17th century for one of the partners in the early mining industry. Look out for the remains of the rails that took the ore-laden trucks from the mines to the smelting mills.

Go through a gate, cross Level House Bridge and go uphill. This track follows the Old Rake Vein, towards the Merryfield Mines. As the climb levels off and another track joins from the left, turn right down a rougher track into the small valley of Doctor Gill. Cross two streams, then climb out on a vague path past spoil heaps and across bare ground with some small cairns. Continue in the same direction across moorland to the corner of a fence, go ahead with the fence on your right, then cross to the other side at a gate. Descend slightly to a stony area, then turn right alongside a stream gully. The track quickly becomes clear. It soon crosses the stream and continues over open moor, descending gently and then climbing equally gently. As it starts to descend again, pass grouse butts and spoil heaps, then fork right at a bare stony area. Follow the obvious track past numerous spoil heaps and shafts.

There are views into Arkengarthdale, another heavily mined area, to the left, and you can see the remains of hushes, an early method of reaching the ore. Above a steep slope a stream was dammed with turf. Once filled, the dam was breached and the water rushing downhill gouged a trench in the slope, with luck exposing the vein.

Keep on down the main track as other tracks join from the right and then left. Just above a road it bends sharp left; bear right on a green track to join the road and go right. Descend to a footbridge beside the ford at Fore Gill Gate (once used in the opening titles of BBC television's *All Creatures Great and Small*) and continue along the road.

Just before completing the walk, you will cross the flue from the old Surrender Smelt Mill, downstream to your left. The flue led to the chimney high up on your right. Such long flues enabled the smelt mills to use higher temperatures to separate the lead from the slag. Some lead vapourises in extreme heat, and the long flues meant that the gases cooled as they went towards the chimney, so the lead solidified in the walls. Men (or often boys) could then be sent into the flues to recover the lead deposit.

Cross the bridge to return to the parking place.

Semer Water – A Legendary Glacial Lake

Legends — perhaps with a basis in dim and distant truth — surround Yorkshire's biggest natural lake.

DISTANCE 5 miles (8km)   MINIMUM TIME 2hrs 15min

ASCENT/GRADIENT 853ft (260m) ▲▲▲   LEVEL OF DIFFICULTY +++

PATHS Field paths and tracks, steep ascent from Marsett, 16 stiles

LANDSCAPE Valley, lake and fine views over Wensleydale

SUGGESTED MAP OS Explorer OL 30 Yorkshire Dales – Northern & Central

START/FINISH Grid reference: SD 921875

DOG FRIENDLINESS Dogs should be on lead

PARKING Car park at the north end of the lake: fee payable at Low Blean Farm nearby

PUBLIC TOILETS None en route

Semer Water was formed as the result of the end of the last ice age. Glacial meltwater attempted to drain away down the valley the glacier had gouged out of the limestone, but was prevented from doing so by a wall of boulder clay, dumped by the glacier itself, across the valley's end. So the water built up, forming a lake which once stretched 3 miles (4.8km) up Raydale. Natural silting has gradually filled the upper part of the lake bed, leaving Semer Water – at 0.5 mile (800m) long North Yorkshire's largest natural lake.

Legendary Semer Water

Semer Water boasts several legends. One concerns the three huge blocks of limestone deposited by the departing glacier at the water's edge at the north end of the lake. Called the Carlow Stone and the Mermaid Stones, they are said to have landed here when the Devil and a giant who lived on Addlebrough, the prominent hill a mile (1.6km) to the east, began lobbing missiles at each other.

More famous is the story of the beggar who came to the town that once stood where the lake is now. He went from door to door, asking for food and drink, but was refused by everyone – except the poorest couple. Revealing himself as an angel, he raised his staff over the town, crying 'Semer Water rise, Semer Water sink, And swallow all save this little house, That gave me meat and drink.' The waters overwhelmed the town, leaving the poor people's cottage on the brink of the new lake. Some say the church bells can still be heard ringing beneath the waters.

Behind the Legend

There are indeed the remains of a settlement beneath Semer Water. Houses perched on stilts were built along the water's edge in Iron Age times, though there may have been an earlier settlement here in neolithic times, too, for flint arrow heads have been found. A Bronze Age spear head was found in 1937 when the lake's waters were lowered.

SEMER WATER

Setts and Quakers

Marsett, at the lake's southern end, and Countersett, to the north, both end with the Old Norse word denoting a place of hill pasture. Marsett is a hamlet of old farmhouses, and on the road to Countersett, at Carr End, is the house where Dr Fothergill was born in 1712.

A famous Quaker philanthropist, he founded the Quaker school at Ackworth in South Yorkshire. The American statesman Benjamin Franklin said he found it hard to believe that any better man than Fothergill had ever lived. Countersett has one of several old Friends' Meeting Houses in Wensleydale, and the Hall was home, in the 17th century, to Richard Robinson, who was responsible for the spread of Quakerism in the Dales.

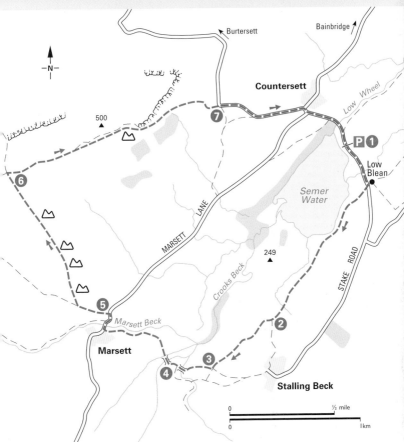

WALK 41 DIRECTIONS

❶ Turn right from the car park up the road. Opposite Low Blean farm, go right over a stile, signed 'Stalling Busk'. Cross another stile and continue towards a barn. Pass right of it to find a clearer path. Follow this, leaving the lake behind and passing a Wildlife Trust sign. Continue past an information board and then skirt above an old graveyard to a gate and signpost just beyond.

❷ Follow the Marsett sign into the field corner and cross a gated stile. Follow the level path through more stiles, then across a larger field, keeping just above a steeper slope. Pass right of a barn among trees, then cross a stream bed.

WHAT TO LOOK OUT FOR

Semer Water offers a wide variety of habitats for wildlife. The waters of the lake, which have a high plankton content, support many fish including bream and perch, as well as crayfish. Water birds include great crested grebe and tufted duck. You may also occasionally see Whooper swans. Over the fringes of the lake, dragonflies and damsel flies can be seen glittering in the summer. On the wet margins of the lake grow flowers such as marsh marigold, marsh cinquefoil, ragged robin and valerian, while in the drier areas the wood anemone is frequently found. Birds such as lapwings, redshank and reed bunting may also be seen, while summer visitors include the sandmartin.

3 Bear right immediately on a narrow path, descending gently above a roofless barn to a stile. Continue to a stile at the corner of another barn, then turn right immediately across a level meadow, with a wall on your right. Cross the wall at a gate, then follow it to a footbridge. Cross and go straight ahead to another footbridge beside a ford.

4 Continue along the obvious track, meeting another river. Approaching Marsett, bear right across a green, following the stream, to a red telephone box. Turn right over the bridge. In 100yds (91m) beyond, take a track signed 'Burtersett and Hawes' (not the path by the river).

5 Walk uphill to a gate on the right where the wire fence ends. Cross the stile and climb a faint

WHILE YOU'RE THERE

Visit Bainbridge, with its wide green and attractive houses. The Romans had a fort here, Virosidum, on top of the hill called Brough. The River Bain, crossed by the bridge which gives the village its name, is England's shortest river, running all of 2 miles (3.2km) from Semer Water to the River Ure.

but direct (and generally steep) path. Reaching a ladder stile with an Access Land symbol, go straight ahead up a final steep slope, then more easily on a green path to a crossing track just below the final crest.

6 Turn right along the track to a gate on the skyline. Continue along the track to a green knoll with views to the west. Descend to a gate, then follow the track more steeply downhill, winding below crags then slanting down the slope on a grooved track. Follow the track as it bends right and back left to reach a road.

WHERE TO EAT AND DRINK

The nearest place to Semer Water is Bainbridge, where the Rose and Crown Hotel by the Green dates back more than 500 years. The Bainbridge Horn, blown to guide travellers to the village in the dark winter months, hangs here. The hotel serves home-cooked local produce both in the bars and, in the evening, in the Dales Room Restaurant.

7 Turn right and follow the road downhill to a staggered crossroads on the edge of Countersett. Turn right, then left, signed 'Stalling Busk'. Descend the lane over the bridge and back to the car park.

A Riverside Circuit High in the Dales

A classic walk in Upper Swaledale from Keld to Muker along Kidsdon Side, and back by the river.

DISTANCE 6 miles (9.7km)   MINIMUM TIME 2hrs 30min

ASCENT/GRADIENT 820ft (250m) ▲▲▲   LEVEL OF DIFFICULTY ✦✦✦

PATHS Field and riverside paths and tracks, 5 stiles

LANDSCAPE Hillside and valley, hay meadows, riverside and waterfalls

SUGGESTED MAP OS Explorer OL 30 Yorkshire Dales – Northern & Central

START/FINISH Grid reference: NY 892012

DOG FRIENDLINESS Dogs on lead (there are lots of sheep)

PARKING Signed car park at west end of village near Park Lodge

PUBLIC TOILETS Keld and Muker

Keld – its name is the Old Norse word for a spring – is one of the most remote of the Dales villages. Set at the head of Swaledale, its cluster of grey cottages is a centre for some of the most spectacular walks in North Yorkshire. This walk follows, for part of its way, the traditional route by which the dead of the upper Dales were taken the long distance for burial in Grinton churchyard. Leaving the village, the walk takes the Pennine Way as it follows the sweep of the Swale on its way down to Muker. This is Kisdon Side, on the slopes of the conical hill known as Kisdon. It was formed at the end of the ice age; the Swale used to flow west of the hill but glacial debris blocked its course and forced it to the east, in its current bed.

Muker and the mines

As the Pennine Way goes west, eventually to climb the slopes of Great Shunner Fell, the walk joins the Corpse Way and descends into Muker. It is worth taking some time to explore the village. Like many Swaledale settlements, it expanded in the 18th and 19th centuries because of local lead mining. The prominent Literary Institute was built for the mining community; though in a nice reverse of fortunes, when the new chapel came to be built in the 1930s, dressed stone taken from the ore hearths at the Old Gang Mine down the valley was used. The Anglican church, which eventually did away with the long journey to Grinton, dates from 1580.

Rocks and Crackpot

Beyond Muker, the walk passes through hay meadows and along the banks of the Swale. Both sandstone and limestone are found in this section; look out for the sandstone bed underlying the river. The limestone of the area is part of the thick Ten Fathom bed, one of the Yoredale series of sedimentary rocks. Where the valley of Swinner Gill crosses the path are the remains of a small smelt mill which served nearby mines. As you ascend the hill beyond, the ruins of Crackpot Hall, a farmhouse long abandoned because of mining subsidence and changes in farming fortune, are to your right. Its name means 'Crows Pothole'.

KELD

As the track descends the valley side, the waterfall of Kisdon Force is below you on the Swale, and there are high overhanging crags on the opposite bank. Further along, you turn downhill to the footbridge over the river, passing East Gill Force. Like all the Dales falls, the volume of its water can vary wildly from the merest summer trickle to a raging winter torrent. Whatever its condition, the rocks around can be very slippery and you should take special care if you leave the path to get a better view.

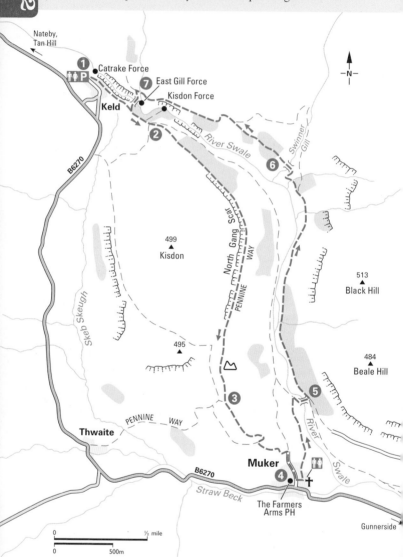

WALK 42 DIRECTIONS

❶ Walk back down the car park entrance road, and straight

ahead down a gravel track, signed 'Muker'. Continue along at the upper level, ignoring a path downhill to the left. Go through a gate, pass a sign to Kisdon Upper Force, and continue along the path below crags to a signpost.

2 Turn right, following the Pennine Way, and go up to a gap in a wall and another signpost. Go left and follow a rough but mostly level path along Kisdon Side, first above woodland then across more open slopes. Cross a ladder stile as the path starts to descend. Go down to a signpost and bear right to another signpost, where the Pennine Way goes right.

3 Bear left down a walled track, marked 'Muker'. The track becomes gravelled and then metalled, finally descending into a walled lane on the edge of the village. Continue to a T-junction.

4 Turn left and in a few paces left again by a sign to Gunnerside and Keld. Follow the paved path through six gates to the river. Turn sharp right and walk downstream to a footbridge.

5 Ascend steps beyond the footbridge and turn left, signed 'Keld'. Follow a clear track up along the valley, until it curves right into Swinner Gill. Cross a footbridge by the remains of lead workings, and go up to a wooden gate.

6 Go straight ahead up the hill and through woodland. The track levels out, then starts to descend, winding left round a barn then swinging back right. Continue steadily downhill to reach a gate above East Gill Force.

7 Fork left by a wooden seat, at a sign to Keld. Follow the path down to a footbridge then bear right, uphill, to a T-junction, where you turn right and follow the track back to the car.

WALK 42

WHERE TO EAT AND DRINK

Muker has a top-notch tea room, attached to the Village Store. Just round the corner, the Farmers Arms provides excellent beer, plus good home-made bar meals in the cosy bar with its open fire. Keld Lodge has a good restaurant.

WHILE YOU'RE THERE

Take the minor road that leaves the B6270 just west of Keld to reach Tan Hill and its inn, the highest in England at 1,732 feet (528m) above sea level. With no neighbouring dwelling for at least 4 miles (6.4km) in any direction, it is as welcome a sight for walkers today as it was for the packhorse-train drivers of the past, and the coal and lead miners who worked on the surrounding moors. It's not advisable to attempt the drive in fog, snow or icy weather.

WHAT TO LOOK OUT FOR

Around Muker, traditional hay meadows are still to be found. They are an important part of the farmer's regime, which is why signs ask you to keep to single file as you walk through them. Such a method of farming helps maintain the wide variety of wild flowers that grow in the hay meadows. The barns, too, are part of older farming patterns, and form one of the most important visual assets of the Dales. The Muker area is especially rich in them – there are 60 within 0.5 mile (800m) of the village. Their purpose was to store the hay after it was cut, to feed the three or four animals who would be over-wintered inside. This was to save the farmer moving stock and hauling loads of hay long distances. It also meant that the manure from the beasts could be used on the field just outside the barn.

Spectacular Landscapes in Limestone Country

*The noble Malham Cove is the majestic highlight
of this quintessential limestone Dales walk*

DISTANCE **6.25 miles (10.1km)**   MINIMUM TIME **3hrs**

ASCENT/GRADIENT **1,148ft (350m) ▲▲▲**   LEVEL OF DIFFICULTY **+++**

PATHS *Well-marked field and moorland paths, more than 400 steps in descent from Malham Cove, 5 stiles*

LANDSCAPE *Spectacular limestone country, including Malham Cove*

SUGGESTED MAP *OS Explorer OL 2 Yorkshire Dales – Southern & Western*

START/FINISH *Grid reference: SD 894658*

DOG FRIENDLINESS *Mostly off lead, except where sheep are present or signs indicate otherwise*

PARKING *At Water Sinks, near gateway across road*

PUBLIC TOILETS *Car park in Malham village*

As you begin this walk, the stream from Malham Tarn suddenly disappears in a tumble of rocks. This is the aptly-named Water Sinks. In spectacular limestone country like this, it is not unusual for streams to plunge underground – it was subterranean watercourses that sculpted the cave systems beneath your feet. As you will see as you continue, this particular stream has not always been so secretive. The now-dry valley of Watlowes just beyond Water Sinks was formed by water action. It was this stream, in fact, that produced Malham Cove, and once fell over its spectacular cliff in a waterfall 230ft (70m) high. Although in very wet weather the stream goes a little further than Water Sinks, it is 200 years since water reached the cove.

Pavement and Cove

Beyond Watlowes valley you reach a stretch of limestone pavement – not the biggest, but probably the best-known example of this unusual phenomenon in the Dales. The natural fissures in the rock have been enlarged by millennia of rain and frost, forming the characteristic blocks, called clints, and the deep clefts, called grikes. It's worth looking closely into the grikes; their sheltered environment provides a home to spleenworts and ferns, and you will sometimes find rare primulas flowering in their shade. The limestone pavement is the summit of the most spectacular of natural features in the Yorkshire Dales – the huge sweep of the cliffs known as Malham Cove. Take care as you explore the pavement, as the edge is not fenced. As you descend the 400-plus steps, the sheer scale of the Cove becomes apparent. It was formed by a combination of earth movement (it is on the line of the Middle Craven Fault), glacial action and the biting away of its lip by the former waterfall.

Fields, Falls and Fairies

On the slopes to the east of Malham Cove you can see ancient terraced fields. Up to 200yds (183m) long, they were painstakingly cut and levelled by Anglian farmers in the 8th century for producing crops. They show how the population was expanding then, and that there was simply not enough farmland on the valley floors to feed everyone. After walking through Malham village, the route passes through fields and a wooded gorge – called Little Gordale – to Janet's Foss. One of the classic waterfalls of the Dales, it is noted for the screen of tufa, a soft, porous limestone curtain formed by deposits from the stream, that now lies over the original lip of stone that was responsible for creating the fall. Janet (or Jennett) was the Queen of the local fairies, and is said to have lived in the cave behind the fall.

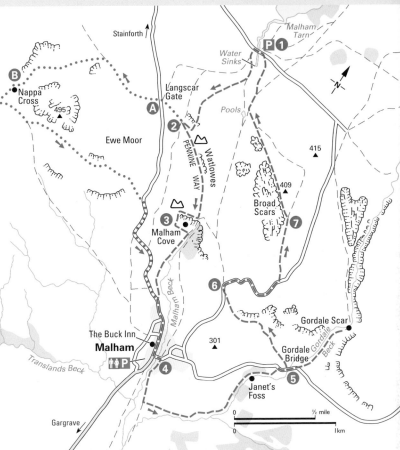

WALK 43 DIRECTIONS

❶ From the car parking space, walk through the gate, then turn left through the kissing gate at the Malham Cove sign. Keep left at the next signpost, following the Pennine Way down the dry valley until the path bends sharp right, overlooking another dry valley.

❷ Turn left, cross a stile and descend steeply into the lower valley. Walk down the level valley to a stile at the end. Just beyond this is the limestone pavement at the top of Malham Cove. Turn right and walk along the pavement. Take great care here, both of the sheer drop down to your left and the gaps in the limestone pavement (known as grikes). Turn left to descend beside a stone wall; go through a gate, then descend more than 400 steps to the foot of the Cove.

❸ At the bottom fork left to visit the very base of the cliff, then follow the obvious track beside the river. On reaching the road, turn left and follow it into the centre of Malham village. Turn left to cross the bridge.

❹ Turn immediately right on a track past some houses then continue along a gravelled path. Follow it left at a sign to Janet's Foss. Eventually the footpath enters woodland, then climbs beside a waterfall (Janet's Foss) to a kissing gate. Turn right along the road, towards Gordale Scar.

❺ At Gordale Bridge (actually two bridges), go through a gate to the left. (To visit Gordale Scar,

continue straight ahead here. Take a signed gate to the left and follow the path through a field into the gorge. Continue as far as the waterfall and then follow the same route back to the bridge.) On the main route, follow the signed public footpath uphill through three gates. Climb alongside a lane before emerging on to it.

❻ Turn right and follow the lane uphill for 600yds (549m), to a ladder stile on the left. Follow a track to a footpath fingerpost.

❼ Bear left and walk over a broad open moor before descending to some small pools. Turn right at a sign for Malham Tarn, go over a ladder stile, take the left-hand path and follow it back to the car park.

Nappa Cross and Malham Cove

This extra loop on Walk 43 avoids the steep climb down Malham Cove, and adds wide views of the surrounding landscape.

See map and information panel for Walk 43

DISTANCE *7.5 miles (12.1km)*   MINIMUM TIME *3hrs 30min*

ASCENT/GRADIENT *1,738ft (530m)* ▲▲▲   LEVEL OF DIFFICULTY +++

WALK 44 DIRECTIONS
(Walk 32 option)

When you reach Point ❷ on Walk 43, don't cross the stile but continue up the valley, then go left over a ladder stile after a few paces. Walk up the field, with a wall on your right, and meet a road by a cattle grid at Langscar Gate, Point 🅐.

Cross the road, go through a gate and follow the grassy track uphill. This is an area with evidence, in the form of earthworks, of Iron Age settlements. Off the path to the right is a typical 'shake hole', often seen marked on maps in limestone country. These are usually seen as hollows or deeper depressions in the sheep-cropped turf, formed when caves under the ground, created by the action of streams, have collapsed. Take care not to walk in the dip – shake holes can be dangerous.

Pass through a gap in a wall, then turn half left by a waymark post, up a grassy track. The track passes through three gates before reaching the stump of Nappa Cross in a wall on the left, Point 🅑. The base and restored post of a medieval monastic cross, Nappa Cross is a reminder that vast areas of the upper Dales were owned by the monasteries and supported the huge flocks of sheep that provided the monks' often vast incomes. Just beyond, opposite a huge cairn, turn left at a bridleway, signed 'Cove Road'. This is part of the former packhorse route from Malham down into Ribblesdale. Malham was an important centre for producing zinc ore, which in the late 18th and early 19th centuries was taken to Gargrave for transportation on the Leeds and Liverpool Canal.

Follow the track through the gate, then downhill to rejoin the road. Turn right and follow the road downhill with views of Malham Cove. Approaching the outskirts of the village, meet the main path to/from Malham Cove to rejoin the main walk at Point ❹.

WALK 45

The Ascent of Pen-y-ghent

To the summit of one of the Three Peaks, and back by the River Ribble.

DISTANCE *6.5 miles (10.4km)*   MINIMUM TIME *3hrs*

ASCENT/GRADIENT *1,555ft (474m)* ▲▲▲   LEVEL OF DIFFICULTY +++

PATHS *Easy-to-follow paths and tracks on Pen-y-ghent. Steep rocky descent from summit, farmland paths, 13 stiles*

LANDSCAPE *One of the Dales' most famous mountains, with spectacular views*

SUGGESTED MAP *OS Explorer OL 2 Yorkshire Dales – Southern & Western*

START/FINISH *Grid reference: SD 808725*

DOG FRIENDLINESS *Dogs should be on lead in farmland*

PARKING *Car park at north end of Horton in Ribblesdale*

PUBLIC TOILETS *At car park*

WALK 45 DIRECTIONS

From the car park, turn right along the road, passing the Pen-y-ghent Café. This is the walkers' centre for the area, selling a vast range of books and maps, and running a booking-in and -out service for those walking or climbing in the area. In 100yds (91m) beyond, turn left, on to a track, following the Pennine Way sign. Go through a gate to a junction of paths and fork left. Follow the walled track for about a mile (1.6km) to its

WHILE YOU'RE THERE

Visit the lively market town of Settle, to the south of Horton in Ribblesdale. If you're there on a Tuesday, you'll find its market in full swing, in front of the impressive arched Shambles building, with two storeys of shops and homes above them. Up the High Street is a large and ornate 17th-century house called The Folly, and scattered through the town are old houses with carved lintels showing when they were built and their builders' initials.

end. (You could detour about 300yds/274m north from here to the huge hole of Hull Pot, which is also easily seen from the upper slopes. In wet weather a stream tumbles down its limestone crags into the depths.)

At the end of the walled track turn right, following the Pen-y-ghent sign to a gate and stiles. Follow an obvious path across level moorland. After another gate, the path climbs again. At a large cairn below limestone crags, the path swings right to slant up a steeper slope. Continue in the same direction on the easier upper slopes until the path swings left to the summit at 2,277ft (694m).

One of the famous 'Three Peaks' of the Dales (the others, Ingleborough and Whernside, are visible from here), Pen-y-ghent's distinctive profile dominates the landscape. Its name, which is Celtic, means either 'the hill on the plain' or 'the windy hill'. Both are appropriate. The ridges that stripe its sides are the result of different rock strata – millstone grit on top, softer shales beneath and, half-way up, a band of limestone. Cross the summit wall and turn right along the stony path, which soon descends very steeply, moving away from the wall at the steepest parts, which have some easy rock scrambling. After the descent you will reach two ladder stiles over a wall on your right. Cross one, following a sign to Brackenbottom. As you descend, the limestone quarry beyond Horton in Ribblesdale is clearly in view. Although National Park policies are weighted against quarry development, many workings often precede the designation of the Dales as a National Park.

Descend steadily, with a continuous wall just to your right, crossing several intermediate walls. Reaching a farm, bear right through a gate and out through another gate to a road. Turn left and follow the road, bearing

WHAT TO LOOK OUT FOR

As you ascend Pen-y-ghent in the spring, you will notice patches of the attractive purple saxifrage growing along the hill's distinctive ridges. Saxifrage means 'stone-breaker', and nearly all the members of the species live in rocky places, their roots penetrating into cracks between the stones to use the moisture trapped there. Purple saxifrage flowers the earliest of all the saxifrages and has five slightly-pointed petals of a delicate purple colour. The tiny flowers form dense clusters among the rocks. As its Latin name (*saxifraga oppositifolia*) suggests, its leaves sit opposite each other along its rather flat stem, which has a creeping habit. A characteristic plant of many high latitudes, the purple saxifrage is the official flower of Nunavut Territory in the very north of Canada.

slightly right as another road joins from the left. Take the next turn right and descend to the main road. Cross and walk down the track opposite. Just before farm buildings, turn right on a short track. Cross stepping stones and keep straight on until the wall on the left ends, then go left over a cattle grid and down a track. Where the track bends left, keep straight ahead beside the stream to a footbridge. Cross this, then bear right across the field, keeping right of an isolated tree, to reach a larger footbridge across the River Ribble.

WHERE TO EAT AND DRINK

The Pen-y-Ghent Café, as well as providing all its other services, does good, energy-giving food, specially geared to the needs of walkers. The village's two pubs, the Crown and the Golden Lion, both offer meals and serve good Yorkshire ales.

You are now joining the Ribble Way, which runs beside the river for 70 miles (113km) from the Dales to the sea. For part of its length, north of Horton in Ribblesdale, it follows the same route as the Dales Way, another long distance footpath that goes the 80 miles (129km) from Ilkley in West Yorkshire to Bowness-on-Windermere in Cumbria.

Cross the bridge and turn right along the river bank. The path follows the river pretty closely, with a slight deviation to cross a stream by a footbridge; there is unusual limestone deposition in the stream bed here. Return to the river bank and keep following it through a bend near houses. Climb steps to a footbridge and cross to return to the car park.

Along the Canal at Gargrave

Following the Leeds and Liverpool Canal from Gargrave.

DISTANCE *3.5 miles (5.7km)*   MINIMUM TIME *1hr 30min*

ASCENT/GRADIENT *114ft (35m)* ▲▲▲   LEVEL OF DIFFICULTY ✤✤✤

PATHS *Field paths and tracks, then canal tow path, 1 stile*

LANDSCAPE *Farmland and canal side*

SUGGESTED MAP *OS Explorer OL 2 Yorkshire Dales — Southern & Western*

START/FINISH *Grid reference: SD 931539*

DOG FRIENDLINESS *Dogs should be on lead, except on the canal bank*

PARKING *Car park near Village Hall, signed from A65*

PUBLIC TOILETS *By bridge in Gargrave*

Gargrave has long been a stopping-off point for travellers from the cities of West Yorkshire on their way to the coast at Morecambe or to the Lake District. These days, most of them arrive along the A65 from Skipton, the route formerly taken by horse-drawn coaches. There is still evidence of the village's importance as a coaching centre, especially at the Old Swan Inn. Its position beside the River Aire had also proved important when 18th- and 19th-century surveyors were seeking westward routes for other methods of transport. The walk crosses the railway not long after leaving Gargrave; this is the route that, not far west, becomes the famous Settle-to-Carlisle line. And you will return to the village beside the Leeds and Liverpool Canal.

Earlier Settlers, Mills and Bandages

Although Gargrave is today mostly a 19th-century settlement, there is evidence that the area has been in occupation much longer. The site of a Roman villa has been identified nearby, while on West Street, excavation has found the remains of a moated homestead dating from the 13th century, with a smithy and a lime pit, that was reused in the 15th century. By the 18th century, there were cotton mills in Gargrave, served by the canal, and weavers were engaged in producing cloth for the clothing industry. Their expertise resulted in the establishment here of one of the village's biggest employers, Johnson & Johnson Medical, where they found workers who could undertake the fine weaving that was needed to produce their bandages.

Canal Digging

In October 1774 the eastern arm of the Leeds and Liverpool Canal, snaking its way westwards from Leeds, reached Gargrave. The route, surveyed by John Longbotham and approved by the great canal-builder James Brindley, had been agreed in 1770. Work began at both the Liverpool and the Leeds ends, but there were, inevitably, arguments between the separate committees in Yorkshire and Lancashire about both the route and the finances.

GARGRAVE

It was not until 1810 that the canal had crossed the Pennines, and barges could go from Leeds to Blackburn, and only in 1816 was the full distance of 127 miles (204km) open to Liverpool. Gargrave benefited not only from the access it gave the village to the raw materials for the cotton mills and the chance to export its cloth, but also as a stopping place for the bargees.

The walk joins the canal near the lowest of the six locks at Bank Newton, where the canal begins a serpentine course to gain height as it starts its trans-Pennine journey. Near the lock is the former canal company boatyard where boats for maintaining the canal were built. As you walk along the tow path, you will cross the Priest Holme Aqueduct, where the canal is carried over the River Aire.

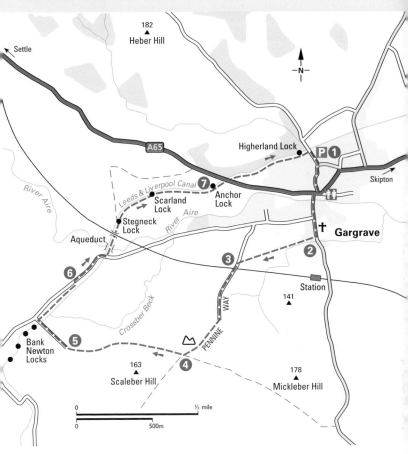

WALK 46 DIRECTIONS

❶ Walk down the lane, past Gargrave Village Hall. At the main road turn right, cross the road and go left into Church Street and over the bridge. Pass the church on your left. Just past Church Close House on your right, turn right, following a Pennine Way sign. Go over a stone stile in the wall on your left.

❷ Turn right along the wall, following the Pennine Way path, which is partly paved here. Go ahead across the field to a waymarked gate, then half left to another gate. Walk up the field, left of power lines, to a gate that leads to a rough sunken lane.

3 Turn left, over a railway bridge, then follow the track up a small hill. Cross a cattle grid, then leave the track to cross a stile on the left into a field. Take a faint path half right then join a track, making for a signpost on the skyline.

4 At the post, turn right to the corner of a wire fence, then slant down a grassy ramp to reach a waymarked gate in a crossing fence. Go ahead across the field to a pair of gates. Take the waymarked left-hand one and continue ahead, at first following a fence and line of trees. Continue straight ahead to meet a track and turn right.

5 Follow the track down to the canal by Bank Newton Locks. Cross the bridge and turn right along the tow path. Where the tow

path runs out, join the lane which runs alongside the canal.

6 Go ahead along the lane, cross the bridge over the canal then turn right down a spiral path to go under the bridge and continue along the tow path. Pass over a small aqueduct over the river, then under a railway bridge. Continue past Stegneck Lock and Scarland Lock to reach Anchor Lock.

7 Beyond the lock, opposite the Anchor Inn, go under the road bridge and continue along the tow path to reach Bridge 170, at Higherland Lock. Go on to the road by a signpost. Turn right down the road, back to the car park.

Erratic Progress

From Austwick along ancient tracks to see the famous Norber Erratics.

DISTANCE	5.5 miles (8.8km)
MINIMUM TIME	2hrs 30min
ASCENT/GRADIENT	558ft (170m) ▲▲▲
LEVEL OF DIFFICULTY	+++
PATHS	Field and moorland paths, tracks, lanes on return, 10 stiles
LANDSCAPE	Farmland and limestone upland
SUGGESTED MAP	OS Explorer OL 2 Yorkshire Dales – Southern & Western
START/FINISH	Grid reference: SD 769683
DOG FRIENDLINESS	Dogs should be on lead
PARKING	Roadside parking near Austwick Bridge and in village
PUBLIC TOILETS	None en route

There is nothing showy about Austwick village. A pleasant, grey-built village, it has several old cottages, many of them dated in the traditional Dales way by a decorative lintel above the main door, showing the initials of the couple who had it built, together with the year they moved in. They mostly date from around the end of the 17th century. On the green in the centre is the restored market cross. The market itself, lost centuries ago to nearby Clapham, has not been restored.

Robin Proctor and Nappa

The walk takes you up Town Head Lane from the village, and across fields into Thwaite Lane. To your left is the ridge of limestone called Robin Proctor's Scar, named after a local farmer whose horse was trained to bring him home after a long night spent in the local pub. One night, too drunk to tell, he mounted the wrong horse, and it plunged over the crag with the farmer on its back. The area below the scar was formerly a tarn, and is now home to a wide variety of marsh plants. Nappa Scar, which the walk passes after you have visited the Norber Erratics, is on the North Craven Fault line. The path goes along a ledge below a steep cliff. In the cliff wall you can see the different strata of rock, including mixed conglomerate and limestone.

The Norber Erratics are world-famous. To geologists they are a place of pilgrimage, and even the non-specialist can tell that something odd is going on here. When you arrive on the plateau above Nappa Scar, you find an extensive grass-covered area, with the remnants of a limestone pavement poking through the tufts. Strewn all over the pavement are grey boulders, some of them of huge size, perched on limestone plinths. These are the erratics. Blocks of ancient greywacke stone, they were carried here from Crummackdale, more than 0.5 mile (800m) away, by the power of a glacier, and dumped when the ice retreated. Over the centuries, the elements have worn down the limestone pavement on which they stand – except where the erratics protected it, resulting in their elevated position.

After you cross Crummack Lane and walk though fields with a limestone ridge and ancient agricultural enclosures, you will reach Austwick Beck, where the water is crossed by an ancient clapper bridge — flat stones laid across the stream from bank to bank. This leads into a walled track that takes you to the hamlet of Wharfe. The route returns to Austwick along other walled lanes. These are the remains of old monastic ways that linked the granges, high on the fells, to the monasteries like Fountains Abbey which owned the vast sheep walks.

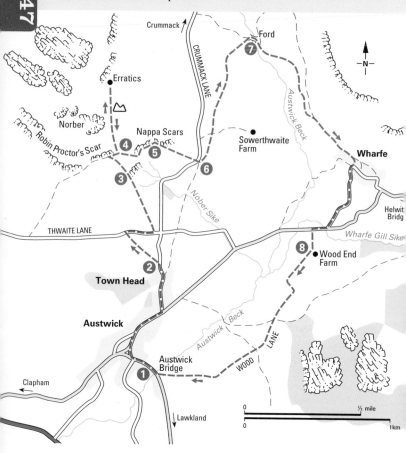

WALK 47 DIRECTIONS

❶ From the bridge, walk through the village. Bear right at the triangular green, following the signpost to Horton in Ribblesdale. Pass the Gamecock Inn and, just past a cottage called Hobbs Gate, turn left up Town Head Lane. Just above the last of the houses, go left over a waymarked ladder stile.

❷ Walk up the field to another stile, and on to another stile on

to a lane. Turn right. Just before reaching a metalled road, turn left over a ladder stile and follow a track. As the track veers left, go straight on, following the stone wall to a stone stile by a gate.

❸ Cross the stile and continue up beside the wall. Where this bends left, by a very large boulder across the path, go right on a track to pass the right-hand edge of the scar. When you reach a signpost, go up left, signposted 'Norber'.

4 Follow the path up on to the plateau, and explore the Norber Erratics. Return the same way, back to the signpost. Turn left, following the sign for 'Crummack'. Follow the green path downhill then back up beside a wall by the scar to a stone stile on your right.

5 Descend to a gap by another stile and follow the path beneath a rocky outcrop. Continue downhill, with a wall on your left, to reach a ladder stile on to a metalled lane. Cross the lane and go over another ladder stile opposite.

6 Turn left across the field. Go over two ladder stiles, cross a farm track and go straight ahead over a rocky ridge to a stone stile. Continue to a gated stile, go left a few paces and then turn right on a track. This soon leads to a ford and clapper bridge.

7 Follow the track between the walls for 0.5 mile (800m) into Wharfe. Turn left at a T-junction in the hamlet, then follow the road round to the right and go down the village approach road to

> ### WHILE YOU'RE THERE
> Clapham village, which stole Austwick's market, has a beck flowing through its centre, and is surrounded by attractive woodland. The village blacksmith at the end of the 18th century was James Faraday, father of the scientist Michael Faraday. From here, too, came the botanist Reginald Farrer, whose name appears in the Latin names of many of the plant species he discovered.

reach a metalled road. Turn right. After 100yds (91m), turn left at a bridleway sign to Feizor, down the road to Wood End Farm.

8 Turn right on a track beside the entrance to the farmyard. Follow it as it bends left and right, then bear right where another track joins from the left. Reaching a crossroads of tracks, go straight ahead, following the line of telegraph poles. The track winds to reach the metalled lane into the village, a few paces from the bridge.

> ### WHERE TO EAT AND DRINK
> The Game Cock Inn in Austwick is a traditional village pub with good ale and food. On the main A65 road just outside the village is the Cross Streets Inn, which has meals at lunchtimes and in the evening. Very much upmarket is the Austwick Traddock, close to the start of the walk: fine dining is the name of the game here.

> ### WHAT TO LOOK OUT FOR
> Nothing is as characteristic of the Yorkshire Dales as its limestone scenery. It is technically known to geologists as a karst landscape – one that has underground drainage, with sinkholes and caves, dry valleys and limestone pavements like those above Crummackdale. Unlike most rocks, limestone is a soluble stone that is constantly being cleaned by the action of rainfall. Soils are not formed, plants do not appear, and the limestone remains pristine in its whiteness. But it is certainly not an unchanging landscape. The glaciers which originally scraped clean the limestone pavements have left their mark elsewhere, in the deep-gouged valleys and in the clefts in the landscape where their meltwaters have torn through the rock. Even more spectacular are the caves under your feet, and the mysterious entrances to them. As you walk through this landscape, stalagmites and stalactite are still being formed beneath your feet.

Around Ribblehead's Majestic Viaduct

Beside and beneath a great monument to Victorian engineering.

DISTANCE 5 miles (8km)	**MINIMUM TIME** 2hrs
ASCENT/GRADIENT 328ft (100m) ▲▲▲	**LEVEL OF DIFFICULTY** +++

PATHS Moorland and farm paths and tracks, 1 stile

LANDSCAPE Bleak moorland and farmland, dominated by the Ribblehead viaduct

SUGGESTED MAP OS Explorer OL 2 Yorkshire Dales – Southern & Western

START/FINISH Grid reference: SD 765792

DOG FRIENDLINESS Dogs can be off lead by viaduct, but should be on lead in farmland

PARKING Parking space at junction of B6255 and B6479 near Ribblehead viaduct

PUBLIC TOILETS None en route

Nowhere in the kingdom has nature placed such gigantic obstacles in the way of the railway engineer', observed a newspaper when the Settle-to-Carlisle railway line was complete. The railway was planned and built by the Midland Railway so it could reach Scotland without trespassing on its rivals' territory of the east or west coast routes. It cost the then enormous sum of £3,500,000 and was opened in 1876. Its construction included building 20 big viaducts and 14 tunnels. At the height of the works, 6,000 men were employed, living in shanty towns beside the line and giving the area a flavour of the Wild West. The line survived for almost 100 years, until passenger services were withdrawn in 1970. It was said that the viaducts, especially the Ribblehead, were unsafe. There was a public outcry which led to a concerted campaign to keep the line open. Since then there has been a change of heart. Ribblehead is repaired, and the line is one of the most popular – and spectacular – tourist lines in the country.

Ribblehead – 'A Mighty Work'

It took all of five years to build Ribblehead's huge viaduct. It is a quarter of a mile (400m) long, and stands 100ft (30m) high at its maximum; the columns stretch another 25ft (7.6m) into the ground. The stone – more than 30,000 cubic yards (22,950 cubic m) of it – came from Littledale to the north, and construction progressed from north to south. The area is called Batty Moss, and was inhospitable, to say the least. There is a rumour that the columns are set on bales of wool, as the engineers could not find the bedrock. This, romantic as it is in a county whose fortunes are largely based in wool, is untrue; the columns are set in concrete on top of the rock below. There are 24 spans, each 45ft (13.7m) wide. Every sixth column is thicker than its neighbours so that if one column fell it would take only five others with it, and the whole viaduct would not fall.

Blea Moor and Ancient Farms

The walk takes you past the viaduct to the beginning of Blea Moor, and near perhaps the most exposed signal box in Britain. Beyond it is Blea Moor tunnel, another of the mighty engineering works of the Settle-to-Carlisle Railway, 2,629yds (2,404m) long and dug by miners working by candlelight. They got through £50-worth of candles each month. The advent of the miners and the huge paraphernalia of Victorian engineering must have seemed astonishing to the farmers sheltering at the foot of Whernside. With their ancient, Norse-inspired names – Winterscales, Broadrake, Gunnerfleet – their farms are an enduring testimony to the resilience of man long before he tried to tame it with such forces.

WALK 48

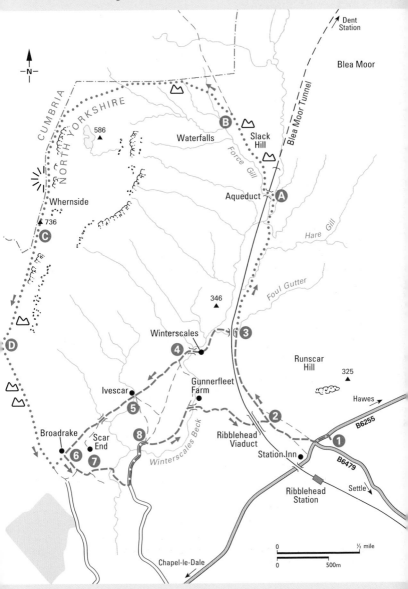

WALK 48 DIRECTIONS

1 From the road junction, with the B6479 at your back, follow green paths towards the viaduct. Turn right on a gravel track and follow it until it turns under the viaduct; continue straight ahead.

2 Walk parallel with the railway line above you to your left, past a Three Peaks signboard. Go through a gate and continue until you reach a railway signal. Go left under the railway arch, following the public bridleway sign.

3 Follow the track downhill towards the stream, then bear left, roughly parallel to the water, to Winterscales. Go through a gate between the buildings and on to a humpback bridge below a cottage.

4 Follow the lane over a cattle grid then fork right (almost straight ahead). Keep left at the next fork, pass an isolated cowshed and continue to Ivescar farm. Pass in front of the house and after a few paces bear left through a waymarked gate.

5 Walk along a track through fields and cross a small bridge of railway sleepers. Immediately after this, bear right to a small gate. Cross a series of fields, keeping a straight course, to reach Broadrake farm.

6 Turn left down the farm track. Where it bends right, go over the cattle grid and turn sharp left round the fence and on to a track, following the bridleway sign, to a ladder stile.

7 The obvious track winds through fields to reach a stream-bed (usually dry in summer). Cross this, which can be tricky after prolonged wet weather. The track is a little indistinct after the crossing, but bear right, staying near the stream until it becomes clear again. Meet a road near a cattle grid, turn left and walk down the road and over a bridge.

8 Where the road divides, go right, through a gate, towards the viaduct. At the next gate, go right again over a footbridge by the farm buildings. Continue along the track and go under the viaduct, then retrace your steps to the parking place.

WHAT TO LOOK OUT FOR

On a fine summer's day Ribblehead can seem a magical place, with the curlews calling, the sheep bleating and the occasional rumble as a train crosses the viaduct – if you're lucky, a steam-hauled one. But it can be one of the bleakest places in the Dales. The average rainfall in the area is 70 inches (177.8cm), but can often be half as much again. Snow frequently blocks the roads. More difficult for the trains, however, is the wind. Wind speeds of 50 knots are a normal occurrence, and gales can reach a greater speed. Crossing the viaduct becomes a hazardous business. The wife of one signalman stationed at Blea Moor was known for walking across the viaduct to catch the train at Ribblehead Station carrying her baby – one hopes that it was calm weather when she attempted the journey.

WHILE YOU'RE THERE

Take the road – or the train – up to Dent Station. You will pass through the Blea Moor tunnel and then over the Dent Head viaduct, with its 10 spans, and the same maximum height as Ribblehead. If you want to visit Dent itself, once in Yorkshire and now adrift in Cumbria, it's a long walk; the station is more than 4 miles (6.4km) from the village!

Ribblehead and Whernside Summit

*If you want to explore the Ribblehead area further, this extension
takes you to the summit of Whernside (2414ft / 736m) and back.*
See map and information panel for Walk 48

DISTANCE 7.25 miles (11.7km)   MINIMUM TIME 3hrs 30min
ASCENT/GRADIENT 1,673ft (510m) ▲▲▲   LEVEL OF DIFFICULTY +++

WALK 49 DIRECTIONS
(Walk 48 option)

At Point ❸ on the main walk, do not turn under the railway arch, but go straight ahead, signposted to Dent. Pass Blea Moor signal box. The obvious stony track crosses over two streams, the first by stepping stones, the second by a footbridge. Just beyond this, cross the railway by a bridge (Point ❹) alongside an aqueduct, where the railway engineers created a new channel to take the waters of Force Gill over the line. Go through a gate, and at a signpost continue ahead for Dentdale (not Dent Head).

This is part of the Craven Way, formerly a packhorse track linking Ribblesdale and Dentdale. The path ascends past a fine waterfall a little way to the left, then climbs steeply to reach a stile on your left, Point ❸.

WHERE TO EAT AND DRINK
In the summer months an ice cream van stations itself at the car park by the road junction, and it's usually there on weekends in winter too for hot drinks and snacks. The Station Inn, near the viaduct, offers warmth (the wind blows at Ribblehead!) and home-cooked meals in its bar and dining room.

Turn left over the stile, following the Whernside sign. The path eventually meets a wall on the right, which is the North Yorkshire county boundary. A paved section leads away from the wall and cuts a corner as it climbs to the ridge. To the right are views of Dent Head viaduct and the ventilation shafts for the Blea Moor tunnel, while further along there are views to the Howgill Fells. Continue along the ridge, keeping the wall on your right, to reach the summit (Point ❻), with its ingenious shelters built into the wall.

Continue along the same path, still keeping the wall on your right, descending easily at first before negotiating two sets of steep, rough steps. Soon the path swings away from the wall, Point ❼. Follow the path steeply downhill to reach two gated stiles over a wall, and continue to a pair of ladder stiles flanking a farm gate. Continue down to a farm gate beside a barn, then turn left, signed 'Winterscales'. Follow the path through the field towards the farm. Go through a gate to reach Point ❻ on the main walk. Turn right down the farm track.

Ingleton and its Famous Waterfalls

A classic Dales walk by the waterfalls,
on a route first devised in 1885.

DISTANCE	5 miles (8km)
MINIMUM TIME	2hrs
ASCENT/GRADIENT	689ft (210m) ▲▲▲
LEVEL OF DIFFICULTY	+++
PATHS	Good paths and tracks, 1 stile
LANDSCAPE	Two wooded valleys with waterfalls, and section of ancient track with wide views
SUGGESTED MAP	OS Explorer OL 2 Yorkshire Dales – Southern & Western
START/FINISH	Grid reference: SD 693733
DOG FRIENDLINESS	Dogs should be on lead by waterfalls
PARKING	Car park in centre of Ingleton
PUBLIC TOILETS	Ingleton

WALK 50 DIRECTIONS

From the main car park in Ingleton, follow the Waterfalls Walk signs, which take you downhill and across the river to the Waterfalls entrance. Pay the hefty entrance fee and walk through the car park to pick up the Waterfalls path. The path undulates, with steps in places.

This is Swilla Glen, which gives a first taste of what to expect on the walk. The River Twiss runs through a deep gorge, with rapids and whirlpools. Cross Manor Bridge and continue upstream. Recross the stream on Pecca Bridge, by Pecca Falls, where the river tumbles over a shelf of the hard greywacke stone, eating away at the softer slate beds below.

Continue upstream, climbing to pass a refreshment hut before reaching Thornton Force. Unlike the other falls on the walk, Thornton Force is not a series of rapids confined within the valley, but plunges 40ft (12.2m) into a deep pool gouged into the slate beds below. This is one of the classic spots for studying the geology of the area. Below the lip of hard limestone are the different strata, including the slates (tipped almost to the vertical by ancient earth movements) and more greywacke. The path winds slightly away from the stream and up steps, then takes you over Ravenray Bridge, and up more steps to a kissing gate on to Twisleton Lane, an ancient packhorse route. Above you are Twisleton Scars, great bands of limestone interspersed

WHILE YOU'RE THERE

Further up the valley, to the north-east of Ingleton, is the hamlet of Chapel le Dale, beautifully set beside the River Greta. Its tiny church – less than 50ft (15m) from end to end – may have been built in the 17th century; no one seems quite sure. In the churchyard are the graves of some of the navvies who died during the construction of the Settle-to-Carlisle Railway.